Department of Economic and Social Affairs
Division for Sustainable Development

TRENDS

IN SUSTAINABLE DEVELOPMENT

Agriculture, rural development, land,
desertification and drought

United Nations
New York, 2008

UN/ST/ESA 2008/15

DESA

The Department of Economic and Social Affairs of the United Nations Secretariat is a vital interface between global policies in the economic, social and environmental spheres and national action. The Department works in three main interlinked areas: (i) it compiles, generates and analyses a wide range of economic, social and environmental data and information on which Member States of the United Nations draw to review common problems and to take stock of policy options; (ii) it facilitates the negotiations of Member States in many intergovernmental bodies on joint courses of action to address ongoing or emerging global challenges; and (iii) it advises interested Governments on the ways and means of translating policy frameworks developed in United Nations conferences and summits into programmes at the country level and, through technical assistance, helps build national capacities.

Note

The designations employed and the presentation of the material in this publication do not imply the expression of any opinion whatsoever on the part of the Secretariat of the United Nations concerning the legal status of any country or territory or of its authorities, or concerning the delimitations of its frontiers. The term "country" as used in the text of the present report also refers, as appropriate, to territories or areas. The designations of country groups in the text and the tables are intended solely for statistical or analytical convenience and do not necessarily express a judgement about the stage reached by a particular country or area in the development process. Mention of the names of firms and commercial products does not imply the endorsement of the United Nations.

United Nations publication
Sales No. E.08.II.A.1
ISBN 978-92-1-104576-5
Copyright © United Nations, 2008
All rights reserved
Printed in United Nations, New York

FOREWORD

Since the United Nations Conference on Environment and Development in 1992 and the subsequent World Summit on Sustainable Development in 2002, significant efforts have been made in pursuit of sustainable development. At the political level, sustainable development has grown from being a movement mostly focusing on environmental concerns to a widely recognized framework utilized by individuals, governments, corporations and civil society that attempts to balance economic, social, environmental and inter-generational concerns in decision-making and actions at all levels. At the September 2005 World Summit, the United Nations General Assembly reiterated that "sustainable development is a key element of the overarching framework for United Nations activities, in particular for achieving the internationally agreed development goals", including those contained in the Millennium Declaration and the Johannesburg Plan of Implementation (General Assembly resolution 59/227).

This report highlights key developments and recent trends in agriculture, rural development, land, desertification and drought, five of the six themes being considered by the Commission on Sustainable Development (CSD) at its 16th and 17th sessions (2008-2009). It notes progress in a number of areas while, at the same time, acknowledging that in other areas significant work is still needed to advance implementation of intergovernmentally agreed goals and targets. A separate Trends Report addresses developments in Africa, the sixth thematic issue under consideration by the Commission.

Department of Economic and Social Affairs
Division for Sustainable Development
April 2008

CONTENTS

INTRODUCTION

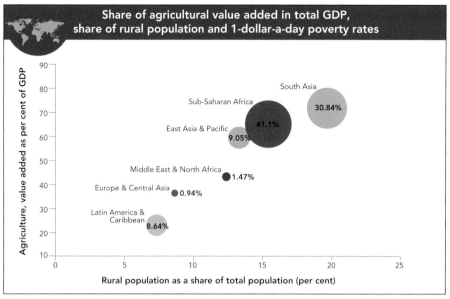

Share of agricultural value added in total GDP, share of rural population and 1-dollar-a-day poverty rates

Source: Poverty rates—Ravallion, Chen and Sangraula (2007); share of agricultural value added and share of rural population—World Bank (2007).

Note: The bubbles represent estimates for 1-dollar-a-day poverty rates in 2004.

Agriculture is key to poverty reduction

Strong agricultural growth has been a consistent feature of countries that have successfully managed to reduce poverty. GDP growth generated in agriculture is, on average, four times more effective in benefiting the poorest half of the population than growth generated outside agriculture, although this effect declines as countries get richer.[1]

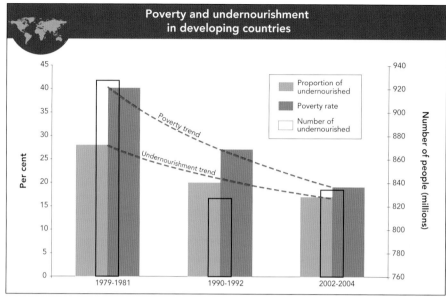

Poverty and undernourishment in developing countries

Source: Poverty rates—Ravallion, Chen and Sangraula (2007); undernourishment rates—FAO (2006).

Note: Dotted lines are logarithmic trends in poverty and undernourishment rates.

Poverty rates have declined more rapidly than undernourishment. Where inequality is high and where a sizeable number of extremely poor people live in relative isolation from the broader economy, those at the bottom of the income scale typically benefit very little from economic growth.[2]

Endnotes

1   World Bank (2007), *World Development Report 2008*.

2   J. Von Braun, A. Patel and W. Soyinka (2007), "Eliminating hunger and reducing poverty: three perspectives", IFPRI 2006-2007 Annual Report Essays, http://dx.doi.org/10.2499/0896299171AR0607E.; and U. Gentilini and P. Webb (2005), "How are we doing on poverty and hunger reduction? A new measure of country-level progress", World Food Programme, mimeo.

Sources for graphs and maps

World Bank (2007), *World Development Indicators 2007*.

M. Ravallion, S. Chen and P. Sangraula (2007), "New evidence on the urbanization of global poverty", Policy Research Working Paper No. 4199, Washington, D.C.: World Bank.

FAO (2006), *The State of Food Insecurity in the World 2006*.

AGRICULTURE

Growth in land and labour productivity, by region, 1971-2003

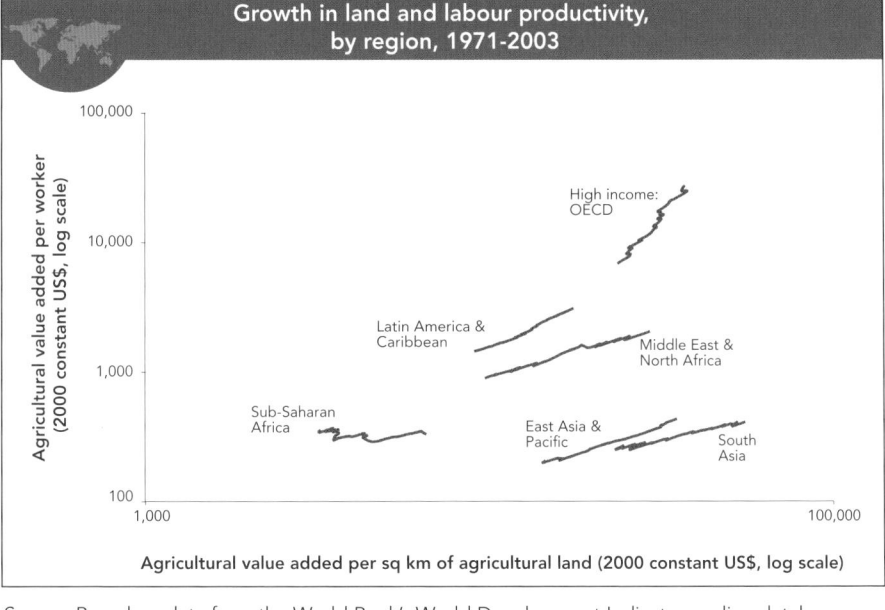

High income: OECD

Latin America & Caribbean

Middle East & North Africa

Sub-Saharan Africa

East Asia & Pacific

South Asia

Agricultural value added per worker (2000 constant US$, log scale)

Agricultural value added per sq km of agricultural land (2000 constant US$, log scale)

Source: Based on data from the World Bank's World Development Indicators online database.

Improvements in agricultural productivity have been fairly widespread, but significant gaps between regions remain

Factors that have driven agricultural land and labour productivity trends include the Green Revolution in Asia, resettlement policies in Latin America, and environmental conservation programmes in developed regions. But a key determinant is the relative scarcity in each region of land, labour and capital. These endowments have favoured investment in land-saving R&D in Asia and labour-saving R&D in North America.

High-income OECD countries with limited supplies of land and labour (especially in Western Europe) show high and increasing land and labour productivity. Asia, with little additional land and abundant labour, has shown high and increasing land productivity but low labour productivity. Sub-Saharan Africa has low productivity in both dimensions, with some limited progress in land productivity but virtually none in labour productivity as its labour force grows rapidly.[3]

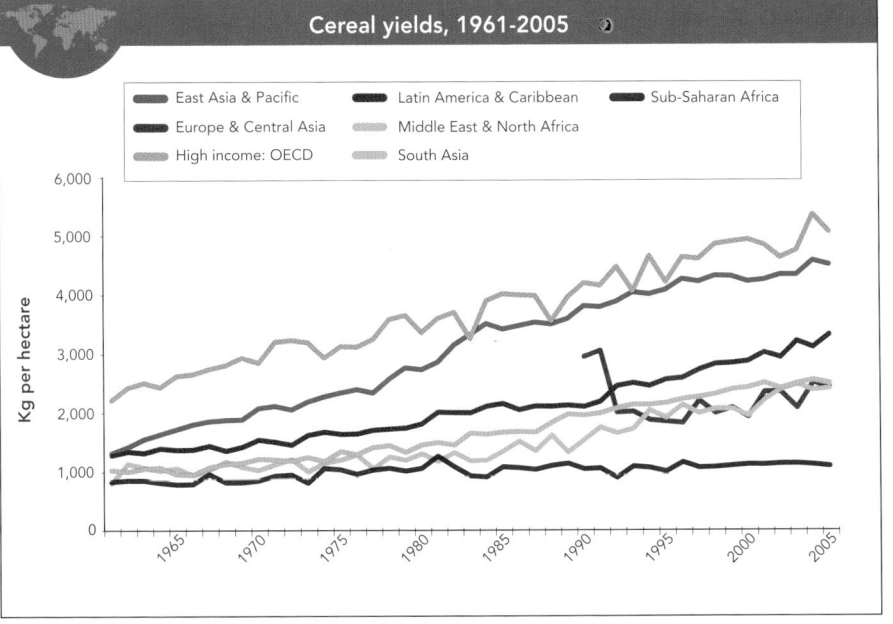

Cereal yields, 1961-2005

- East Asia & Pacific
- Europe & Central Asia
- High income: OECD
- Latin America & Caribbean
- Middle East & North Africa
- South Asia
- Sub-Saharan Africa

Kg per hectare

1965 1970 1975 1980 1985 1990 1995 2000 2005

Source: World Development Indicators online database.

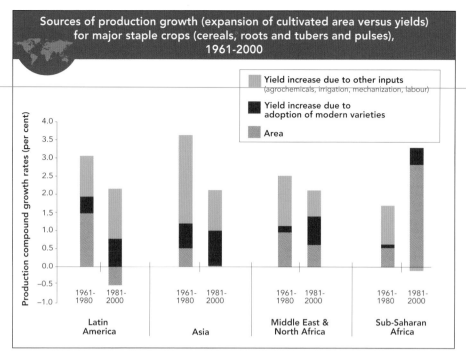

Sources of production growth (expansion of cultivated area versus yields) for major staple crops (cereals, roots and tubers and pulses), 1961-2000

Source: Evenson and Gollin (2003).

Improved varieties have been a major contributor to growth in staple crop production in the developing world, except in Africa

Many farmers around the world, and particularly in Africa, still grow mostly food staples for their own consumption and to supply domestic and regional markets.

In contrast to the rest of the developing world, production growth in sub-Saharan Africa since 1981 was based almost entirely on extending the area under cultivation. The limited scope of the Green Revolution in sub-Saharan Africa was in part due to the mix of crops grown, in part due to difficulties in producing improved varieties suitable for local growing conditions in the region. Varietal improvements have begun to make an impact in rice, maize, cassava and other crops, with public institutions acting as key facilitators of innovation and diffusion.[4]

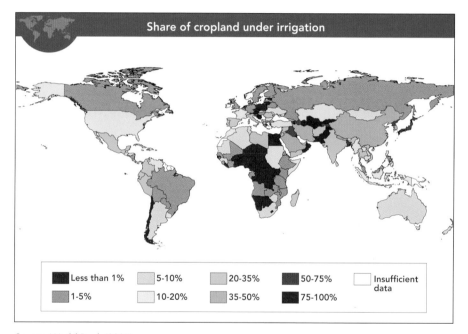

Share of cropland under irrigation

Less than 1% | 5-10% | 20-35% | 50-75% | Insufficient data
1-5% | 10-20% | 35-50% | 75-100%

Source: World Bank (2007).

Irrigation is far more extensive in Asia than in sub-Saharan Africa

Irrigation can lead to improvements in farm income through increased yields and/or diversification into higher-value crops. In Asia, low-potential, rain-fed regions consistently show the highest returns to irrigation. This suggests that there are potentially high returns to investments in irrigation in parts of Africa where irrigation is still extremely limited. Irrigation development in Africa could also contribute significantly to reducing income volatility and alleviating poverty, as rural poverty is dominated by smallholders.[5]

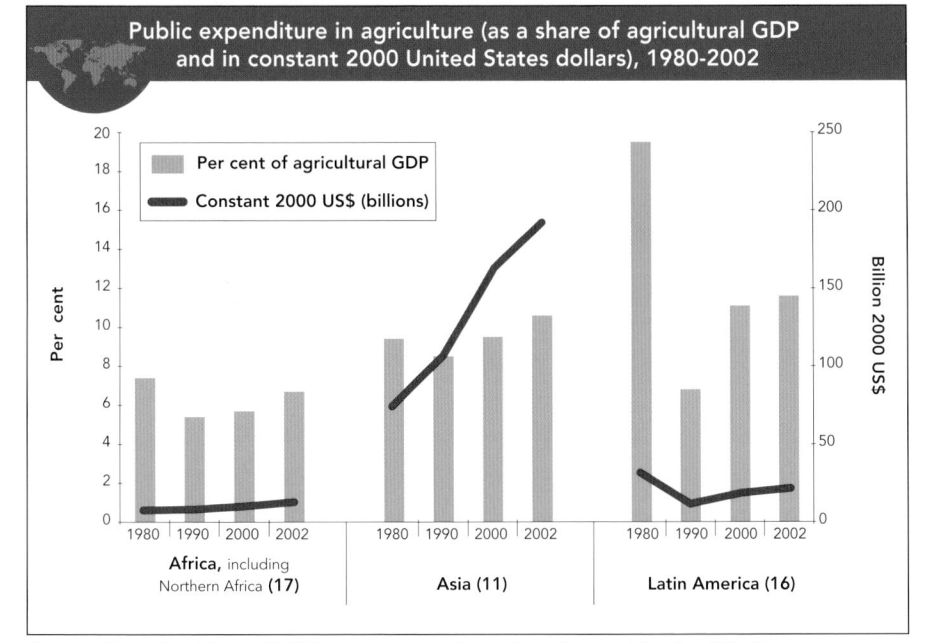

Public expenditure in agriculture (as a share of agricultural GDP and in constant 2000 United States dollars), 1980-2002

Source: Akroyd and Smith (2007) on the basis of data from Fan and Saurkar (2006).

Note: Numbers in parentheses correspond to number of countries in the sample for each region.

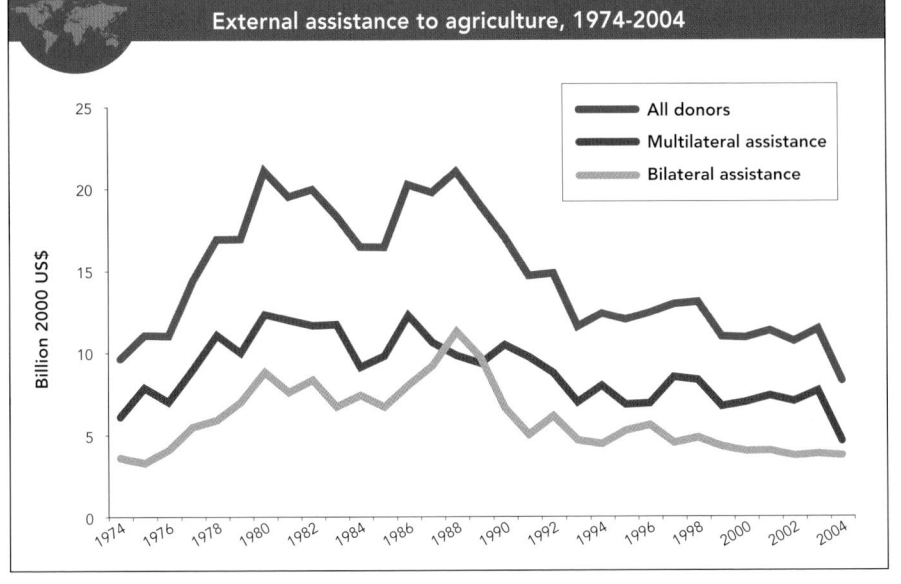

External assistance to agriculture, 1974-2004

Source: Based on FAOSTAT data.

Note: Current United States dollar values were deflated using the United States GDP deflator from the World Development Indicators online database. "External assistance to agriculture" does not include food aid and other technical cooperation provided in kind. The term "agriculture" is used in a broad sense to include forestry, fisheries and rural development.

Only in developing Asia has public spending on agriculture risen steeply over the past generation

In many African countries, spending on agriculture relative to GDP is well below the target set by the 2003 Maputo Declaration of Heads of State and Government of the African Union, which establishes that 10 per cent of budgetary allocations should go to agriculture and rural development by 2008.

Only in Asia has spending increased relative to GDP over the 1980-2002 period, as the result of a near tripling in real terms. The relative decline is most dramatic in Latin America, the only region where expenditures declined in absolute terms, although there has been a recovery between 1990 and 2002.[6]

External assistance to agriculture has been on the decline since the 1980s

A number of studies show positive growth and poverty reduction effects from public spending in agriculture and rural development. At the same time, many low-income countries depend on external assistance for agriculture.[7] Yet, external commitments in real terms have steadily declined since the 1980s. Multilateral assistance has declined proportionately much more than bilateral assistance.

> **Feeding the majority of the poor and vulnerable populations in Africa, while preserving the natural resource base and the environment, is one of the most pressing development challenges of the twenty-first century.**
>
> —Akin Adesina, AGRA

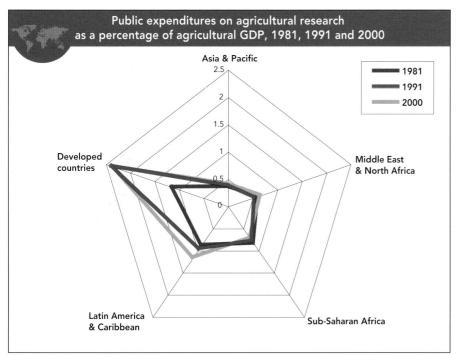

Public expenditures on agricultural research as a percentage of agricultural GDP, 1981, 1991 and 2000

- 1981
- 1991
- 2000

Source: Pardey and others (2006).

Note: Data are estimates and exclude Eastern Europe and the countries of the former Soviet Union.

Developing countries now spend more in total on agricultural R&D than developed countries, but most takes place in only three countries: China, India and Brazil

While there is a large private presence in developed countries, in developing countries the private sector accounted for only 6 per cent of total R&D spending in agriculture as of 2000 (as opposed to over 50 per cent in developed countries) and generally targeted export crops.

In 2000, developed countries as a group spent US$ 2.4 on public agricultural R&D for every US$ 100 of agricultural output, over four times more than in developing regions. In the latter, research intensities have risen somewhat in the past two decades, with the exception of Africa where the intensity has declined.[8]

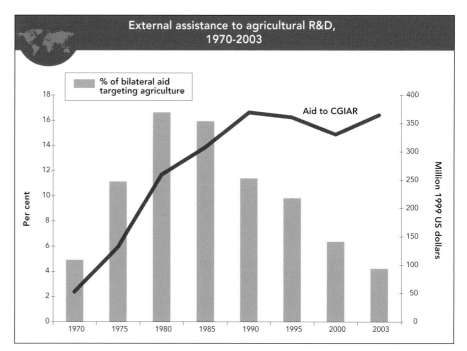

External assistance to agricultural R&D, 1970-2003

- % of bilateral aid targeting agriculture
- Aid to CGIAR

Source: Pardey and others (2006).

Note: CGIAR is the Consultative Group on International Agricultural Research.

Agricultural R&D in developing countries, especially in Africa, has suffered from shifting donor priorities

Development assistance has been an important source of funding for agricultural R&D, including through sponsorship of CGIAR (Consultative Group on International Agricultural Research) research and in underwriting national R&D efforts in some developing countries. Since the 1980s, however, there has been a strong shift away from agriculture in bilateral aid funding priorities. As a share of all bilateral assistance, agriculture fell from over 16 per cent in 1980 to only 4 per cent in 2003. CGIAR funding, which was pivotal in developing Green Revolution technologies, grew markedly from the 1970s but has been stagnant since 1990.[9]

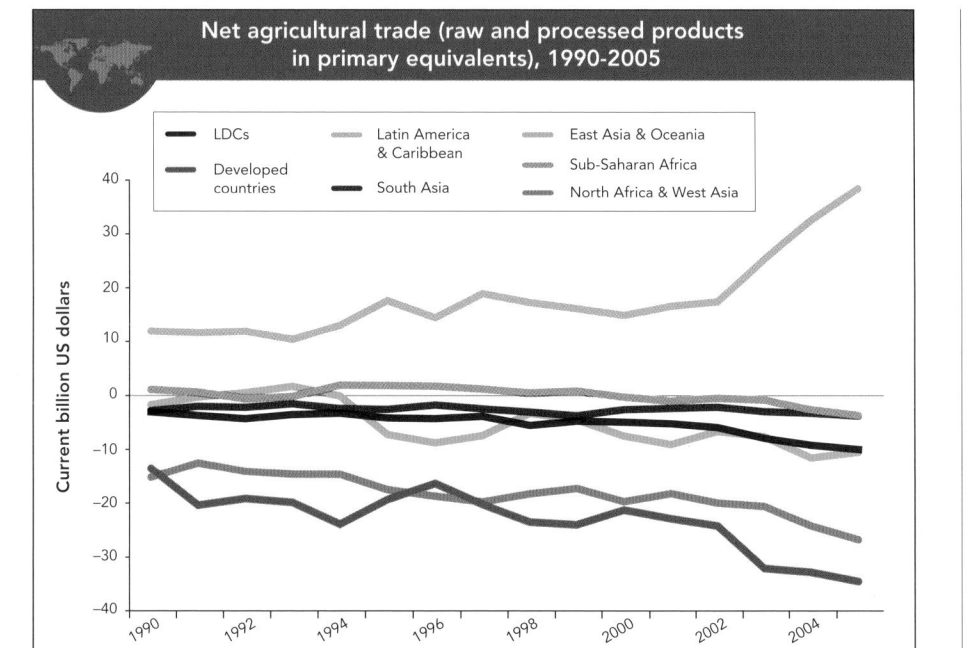

Net agricultural trade (raw and processed products in primary equivalents), 1990-2005

Legend: LDCs; Developed countries; Latin America & Caribbean; South Asia; East Asia & Oceania; Sub-Saharan Africa; North Africa & West Asia

Source: Based on FAOSTAT data and country classifications.

Note: Developed countries include countries with economies in transition.

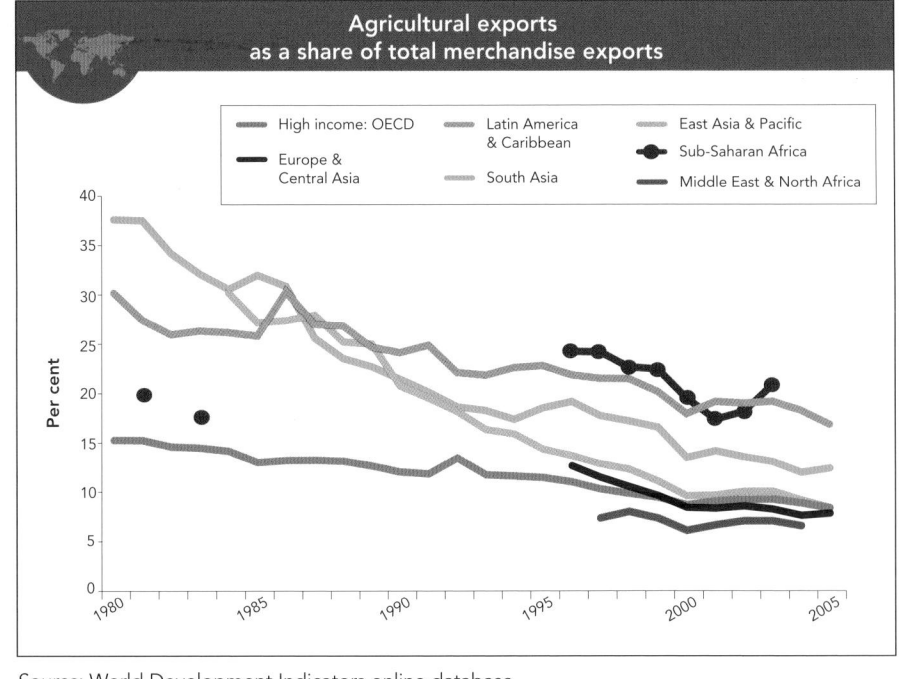

Agricultural exports as a share of total merchandise exports

Legend: High income: OECD; Europe & Central Asia; Latin America & Caribbean; South Asia; East Asia & Pacific; Sub-Saharan Africa; Middle East & North Africa

Source: World Development Indicators online database.

Note: Agricultural exports share = Share of agricultural raw materials exports + share of food exports.

Latin America stands out as a large and fast-growing net agricultural exporter

Latin America and the Caribbean has seen a widening of its agricultural trade surplus, starting around the mid-1990s. Conversely, East Asia and Oceania and sub-Saharan Africa have become net agricultural importers, while the deficit of Northern Africa and West Asia shows no signs of diminishing. The same holds for developed countries as a group. By the end of the 1990s, LDC imports were more than twice as high as exports.[10]

> **More countries are contesting agricultural export markets and have increased their competitiveness and their share of the market.**

Reliance on agricultural exports has been declining globally but remains high in some regions of the developing world

The downward trend has been particularly pronounced in South Asia and East Asia and the Pacific, where on average reliance on agricultural exports is on a par with OECD countries. While less pronounced, in Latin America the share of agricultural exports in total merchandise exports has declined by roughly half over the past quarter-century. In sub-Saharan Africa, that share was only slightly reduced from 1980 to 2005. These regional averages mask large differences between countries and are strongly influenced by the specialization pattern in the largest economies (e.g., Brazil and Mexico in Latin America; China and India in Asia).

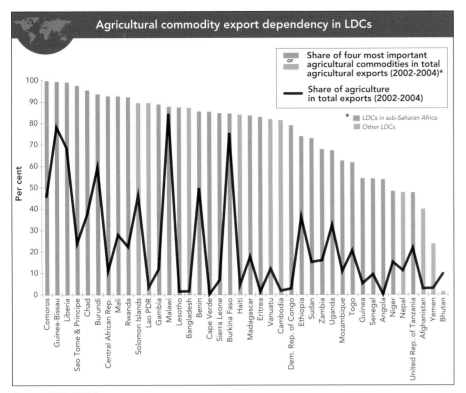

Agricultural commodity export dependency in LDCs

Legend:
Share of four most important agricultural commodities in total agricultural exports (2002-2004)*

Share of agriculture in total exports (2002-2004)

* LDCs in sub-Saharan Africa
Other LDCs

Source: FAO (2006).

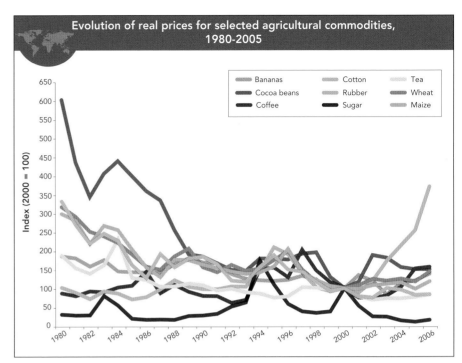

Evolution of real prices for selected agricultural commodities, 1980-2005

Legend: Bananas, Cocoa beans, Coffee, Cotton, Rubber, Sugar, Tea, Wheat, Maize

Source: Based on IMF (2007) data for commodity prices.

Note: Nominal values deflated using the United States Consumer Price Index from the World Development Indicators database. Sugar prices are free market prices.

Commodity-exporting LDCs specialize in a narrow range of primary agricultural commodities

Agricultural productivity in LDCs tends to be lower than in other developing countries, and productivity growth has been too slow to offset the negative effects of falling and volatile commodity prices. In some of their traditional exports, commodity-exporting LDCs are losing market share, and diversification into more dynamic sectors and upgrading into higher value added segments of agricultural commodity production are occurring very slowly.[11]

Growing world food and biofuels demand as well as high oil prices have pushed up the prices of some agricultural commodities since 2000, but not enough to reverse the longer-term downward trend

Government subsidies and other policy support to biofuels have been expanding, putting price pressure on such inputs as maize, palm oil and sugar cane—the last sustained in addition by the 2006 reform of the EU sugar regime.

Other commodities of importance to low-income developing countries, such as cocoa, coffee and cotton, have also benefited from dynamic global demand. In the case of cotton, however, significant distortions in world market prices remain as a result of insufficient subsidy reforms in large exporting countries.[12]

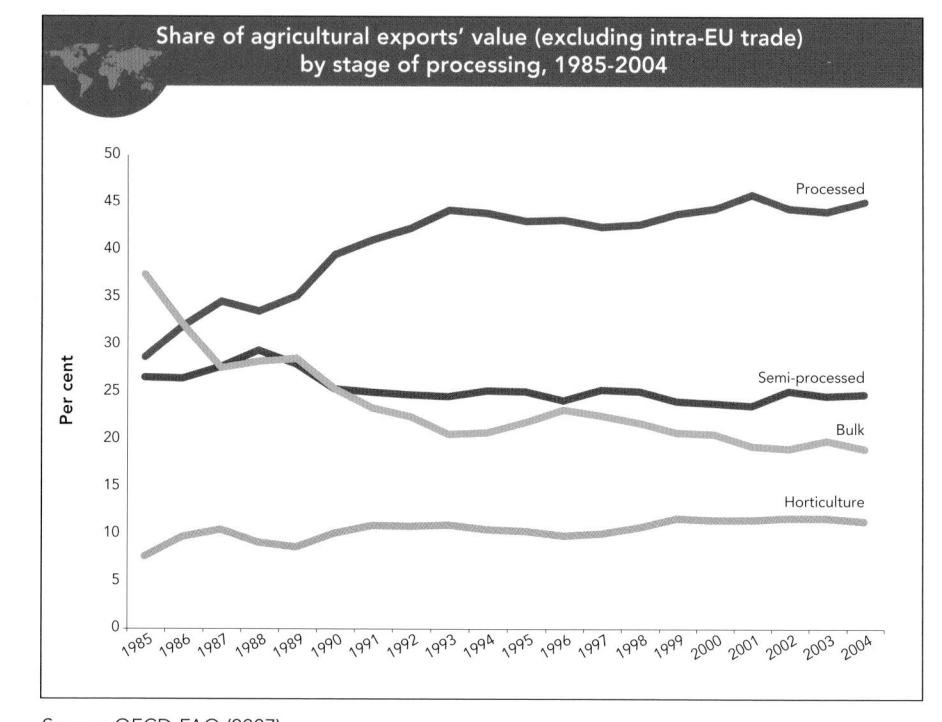

Share of agricultural exports' value (excluding intra-EU trade) by stage of processing, 1985-2004

Source: OECD-FAO (2007).

Processed foods and horticultural products have been highly dynamic in global markets

In the food industry, numerous new products and brands are brought to market every year, as are products with higher quality and service content. Over the past two decades, such highly processed products have enjoyed an average annual growth of 9 per cent, comparable to the growth rate of total merchandise exports. As a result, this group of commodities has steadily increased its share of agriculture trade, to 45 per cent of total exports.

Although from a lower base, horticultural products have increased their market share by nearly half over the past twenty years, as a result of innovations in inputs, post-harvest treatments, packing, labelling, logistics, and the use of specialized skills (e.g., in the introduction and adaptation of new varieties to local conditions).[13]

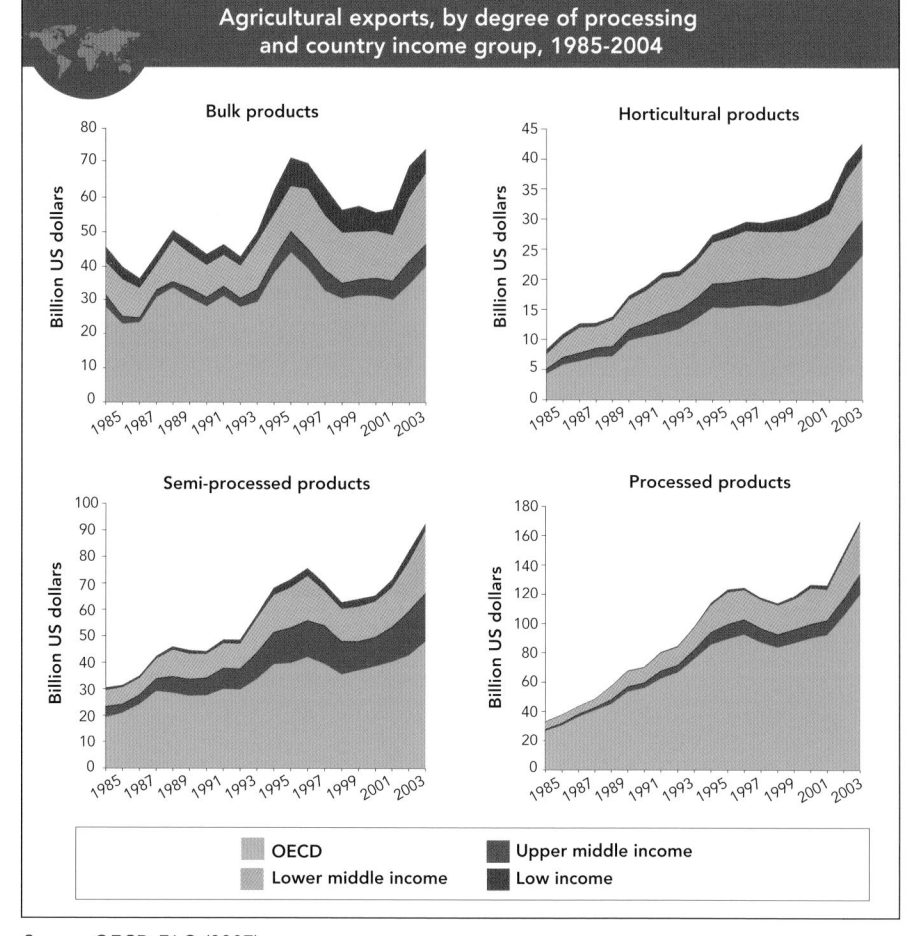

Agricultural exports, by degree of processing and country income group, 1985-2004

Source: OECD-FAO (2007).

Developed countries still dominate world agricultural trade, but middle-income countries have been gaining ground in dynamic product categories

OECD countries are still dominant players in world agricultural trade across categories, and particularly for processed products, the production of which relies on the availability of specialized skills. There are, however, some noticeable structural changes. Exports of processed products by middle-income countries grew at double-digit rates between 1985 and 2004. Those countries also saw rapid growth in their horticultural exports, though the OECD countries still dominate.[14]

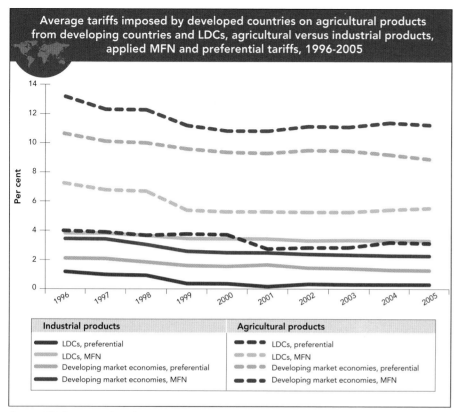

Average tariffs imposed by developed countries on agricultural products from developing countries and LDCs, agricultural versus industrial products, applied MFN and preferential tariffs, 1996-2005

Industrial products
- LDCs, preferential
- LDCs, MFN
- Developing market economies, preferential
- Developing market economies, MFN

Agricultural products
- LDCs, preferential
- LDCs, MFN
- Developing market economies, preferential
- Developing market economies, MFN

Source: UNCTAD, WTO and ITC (2006).

Note: A fixed trade structure has been used to compute the weighted average of tariffs. Agricultural products comprise plant and animal products, including tree crops but excluding timber and fish products.

Developing country agricultural exports still face significant tariff barriers and tariff escalation in developed country markets, although LDCs benefit from substantial preferences

Tariff escalation is only one factor limiting the capture of value added by developing countries. Another is the high market concentration on the buyers' side of agricultural commodity markets and the high fragmentation on the developing country producers' side. Supporting product differentiation through branding and other value-adding activities, on the one hand, and strengthening extension services for smaller producers, on the other, have been tried with success in some countries as a way to overcome these challenges (e.g., the recent trademarking of specialty coffee in Ethiopia).[15]

LDCs face less steep tariff escalation but also generally have less capacity to integrate into processing. Moreover, for those countries benefiting from preferential treatment under the EU's Everything But Arms (EBA) scheme and similar schemes, multilateral liberalization could result in losing market share in favour of more competitive producers, at least for some products.

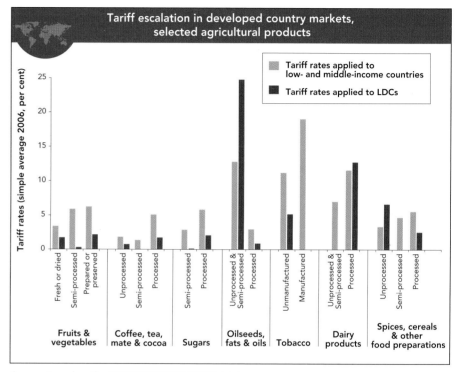

Tariff escalation in developed country markets, selected agricultural products

Legend:
- Tariff rates applied to low- and middle-income countries
- Tariff rates applied to LDCs

Source: Based on the WITS UNCTAD-TRAINS database.

Note: Averages include both ad valorem tariffs and ad valorem equivalents (AVEs) of non–ad valorem tariffs, computed jointly by UNCTAD and the World Bank.

> **The demand for high-value primary and processed products is rapidly increasing, driven by rising incomes, faster urbanization, liberalized trade, foreign investment, and advancing technology.**

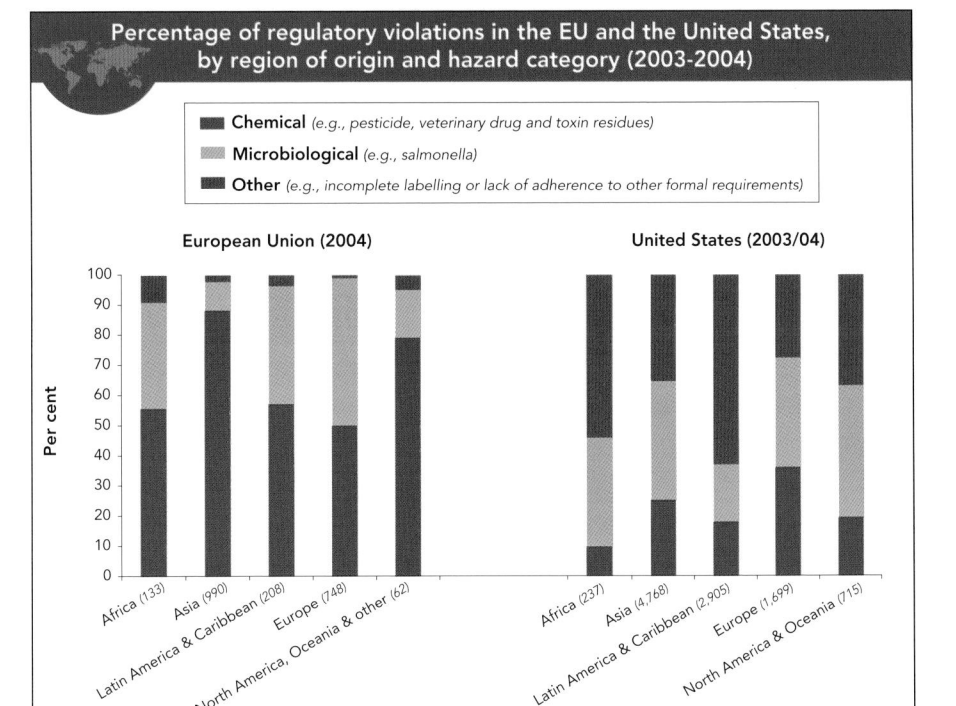

Percentage of regulatory violations in the EU and the United States, by region of origin and hazard category (2003-2004)

- ■ **Chemical** *(e.g., pesticide, veterinary drug and toxin residues)*
- ▨ **Microbiological** *(e.g., salmonella)*
- ■ **Other** *(e.g., incomplete labelling or lack of adherence to other formal requirements)*

European Union (2004)

United States (2003/04)

Per cent

Africa (133)
Asia (990)
Latin America & Caribbean (208)
Europe (748)
North America, Oceania & other (62)

Africa (237)
Asia (4,768)
Latin America & Caribbean (2,905)
Europe (1,699)
North America & Oceania (715)

Source: Wiig and Kolstad (2005) with data from the European Union Rapid Alert System for Food and Feed (RAASF) and the United States Food and Drug Administration (FDA).

Note: Numbers in parentheses refer to the total number of violation notifications.

Many developing countries have weak domestic capacities to meet increasingly demanding product standards

Sanitary and phytosanitary (SPS) measures affect fish and meat products, fruits and vegetables. Prepared foodstuffs and beverages are notably affected by marking, labelling and packaging requirements.[16]

While horticultural, fish and meat products have generally proved to be rewarding markets for developing country producers, stringent sanitary and traceability requirements are driving many smaller producers out of export markets.

The impact of SPS requirements on exports of agricultural and food products can be seen from data on actions taken by the food safety authorities of importing countries. There is considerable variation across both importing and exporting regions in the types of problems identified. Because of the wider scope of the United States FDA system—which (unlike the European Union system) includes notifications for products that are not a direct human health hazard—violations on account of, for example, incomplete labelling account for a larger share of the United States total. Besides different rules and practices in the European Union and the United States, differences in types of notification also reflect different import patterns and can inform the allocation of technical assistance to developing countries.[17]

> **"Enhanced capacity to comply with stricter standards can provide the basis for more sustainable and profitable agro-food exports in the long term."**

Endnotes

3   Millennium Ecosystem Assessment (2005), "Ecosystems and human well-being: current state and trends: Findings of the Condition and Trends Working Group", http://www.millenniumassessment.org/en/Condition.aspx.

4   D. Diao, P. Hazell, D. Resnick and J. Thurlow (2007), "The role of agriculture in development: implications for sub-Saharan Africa", Research report 153, IFPRI; R. E. Evenson and D. Gollin (2003), "Assessing the impact of the Green Revolution", *Science*, 300, May; and E. Z. Gabre-Madhin and S. Haggblade (2004), "Successes in African agriculture: results of an expert survey", *World Development*, vol. 32 (5), pp. 745-766.

5   FAO (2003). Preliminary review of the impact of irrigation on poverty with special emphasis on Asia, AGL/MISC/34/2003, ftp://ftp.fao.org/agl/aglw/docs/misc34.pdf.

6   S. Akroyd and L. Smith (2007), "Review of public spending to agriculture", a joint DFID/World Bank study, Oxford Policy Management, January.

7   S. Akroyd and L. Smith (2007), "Review of public spending to agriculture", a joint DFID/World Bank study, Oxford Policy Management, January.

8   P. G. Pardey, J. M. Alston and R. R. Piggott (2006), *Agricultural R&D in the Developing World: Too Little, Too Late?*, Washington, D.C.: IFPRI.

9   P. G. Pardey, N. M. Beintema, S. Dehmer and S. Wood (2006), *Agricultural Research: A Growing Global Divide?*, IFPRI Food Policy Report, Washington, D.C.: IFPRI.

10 FAO (2006), *The State of Food and Agriculture 2006*.

11 UNCTAD (2002), *The Least Developed Countries Report*.

12 World Bank (2007), Commodity markets overview, May, http://go.worldbank.org/T8EPPB6880.

13 OECD-FAO (2007), *Agricultural Outlook 2007-2016*.

14 OECD-FAO (2007), *Agricultural Outlook 2007-2016*.

15 C. Dolan, J. Humphrey and C. Harris-Pascal (1996), "Horticulture commodity chains: the impact of the UK market on the African fresh vegetable industry", Institute of Development Studies, University of Sussex, United Kingdom; R. Fitter and R. Kaplinsky (2001), "Who gains from product rents as the coffee market becomes more differentiated? A value chain analysis", Institute of Development Studies, University of Sussex, United Kingdom; and C. L. Gilbert (2006), "Value chain analysis and market power in commodity processing with application to the coffee and cocoa sectors", Discussion Paper No. 5, Universitá degli studi di trento—dipartimiento de economia, Italy.

16 OECD (2005), *Looking Beyond Tariffs: The Role of Non-Tariff Barriers in World Trade: Non-Tariff Barriers of Concern to Developing Countries*, Trade Policy Studies.

17 S. Henson and R. Loader (2001), "Barriers to agricultural exports from developing countries: the role of sanitary and phytosanitary requirements", *World Development*, 29(1), pp. 85-102; H. L. Kee, A. Nicita and M. Olarreaga (2006), "Estimating trade restrictiveness indices", Policy Research Working Paper, Series 3840, World Bank; and A. Wiig and I. Kolstad (2005), "Lowering barriers to agricultural exports through technical assistance", *Food Policy*, 30, pp. 185-204.

Sources for graphs and maps

World Development Indicators online database, http://devdata.worldbank.org/dataonline.

R. E. Evenson and D. Gollin (2003), "Assessing the impact of the Green Revolution", *Science*, 300, May.

World Bank (2007), World Development Indicators CD-ROM.

S. Akroyd and L. Smith (2007), "Review of public spending to agriculture", a joint DFID/World Bank study, Oxford Policy Management, January.

S. Fan and A. Saurkar (2006), "Public spending in developing countries: trends, determination and impact", mimeo.

FAOSTAT, http://faostat.fao.org/default.aspx.

World Development Indicators online database, http://devdata.worldbank.org/dataonline.

P. G. Pardey, J. M. Alston and R. R. Piggott (2006), *Agricultural R&D in the Developing World: Too Little, Too Late?*, Washington, D.C.

FAO (2006), *The State of Agricultural Commodity Markets 2006*.

IMF (2007), *International Financial Statistics 2007*.

World Development Indicators online database, http://devdata.worldbank.org/dataonline.

OECD-FAO (2007), *Agricultural Outlook 2007-2016*.

UNCTAD, WTO and ITC (2006), Market Access Indicators, http://www.mdg-trade.org.

WITS UNCTAD-TRAINS database, http://wits.worldbank.org.

A. Wiig and I. Kolstad (2005), "Lowering barriers to agricultural exports through technical assistance", *Food Policy*, 30, pp. 185-204.

Sources for quotes

T. Schultz (1979), "The economics of being poor", Nobel Prize Lecture, http://nobelprize.org/nobel_prizes/economics/laureates/1979/schultz-lecture.html.

A. Adesina (2007), Vice President for Policy and Partnerships, Alliance for a Green Revolution in Africa (AGRA), http://www.rockfound.org/about_us/news/2007/1002black_caucus.shtml.

OECD-FAO (2007), *Agricultural Outlook 2007-2016*, p. 43.

World Bank (2007), *World Development Report 2008*, p. 118.

World Bank (2007), *World Development Report 2008*, p. 130.

RURAL DEVELOPMENT

Rural and urban population, 1950-2030

Legend:
- Share of rural population in less developed regions
- Share of rural population in developed regions
- Rural population (less developed regions)
- Urban population (less developed regions)
- Rural population (developed regions)
- Urban population (developed regions)

(Y-axis left: Millions — 0, 500, 1,000, 1,500, 2,000, 2,500, 3,000, 3,500, 4,000, 4,500)
(Y-axis right: Per cent — 0, 10, 20, 30, 40, 50, 60, 70, 80, 90)
(X-axis: 1950, 1955, 1960, 1965, 1970, 1975, 1980, 1985, 1990, 1995, 2000, 2005, 2010, 2015, 2020, 2025, 2030)

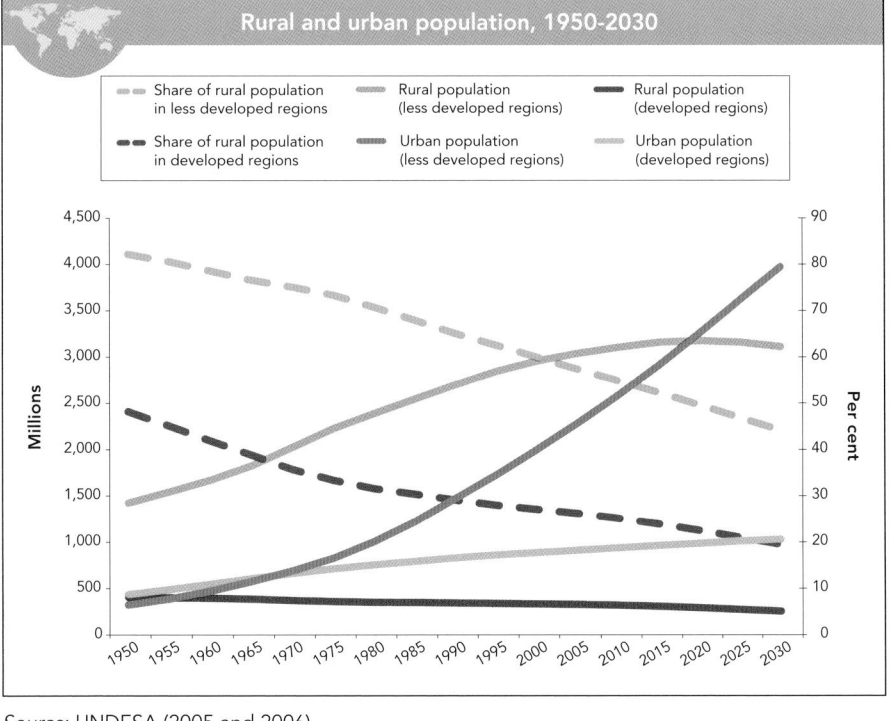

Source: UNDESA (2005 and 2006).

Note: Developed regions comprise all regions of Europe plus Northern America, Australia/New Zealand and Japan; less developed regions comprise all regions of Africa, Asia (excluding Japan), Latin America and the Caribbean plus Melanesia, Micronesia and Polynesia.

Population in developing regions will remain predominantly rural until 2020

After that, the size of the rural population is expected to decline due to slower population growth and rapid urbanization in most countries.

The share of the population living in rural areas is declining on all continents, although it is projected to remain above 50 per cent in South and Central Asia and sub-Saharan Africa until 2030.[18]

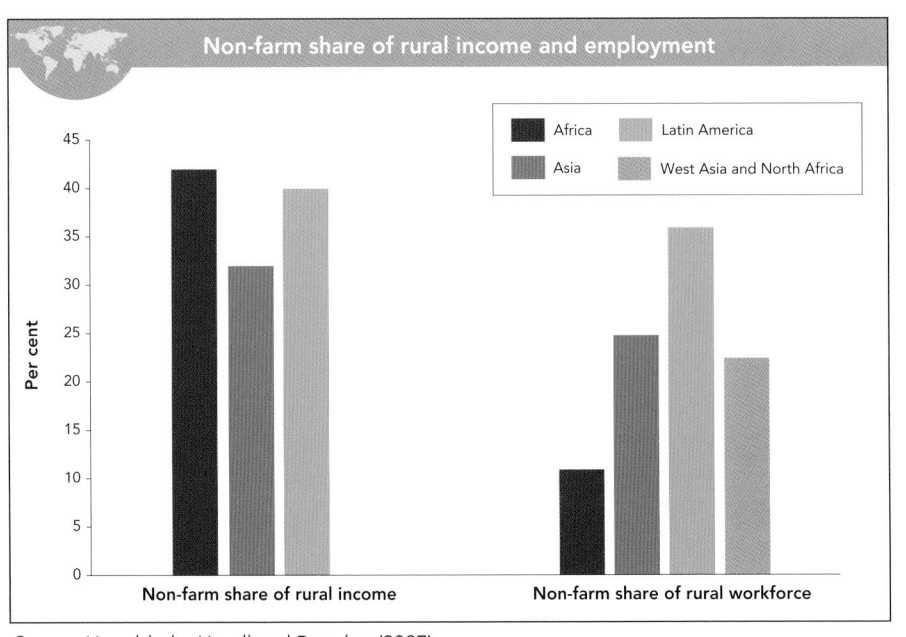

Non-farm share of rural income and employment

Legend:
- Africa
- Asia
- Latin America
- West Asia and North Africa

(Y-axis: Per cent — 0, 5, 10, 15, 20, 25, 30, 35, 40, 45)
(Categories: Non-farm share of rural income, Non-farm share of rural workforce)

Source: Haggblade, Hazell and Reardon (2007).

Note: Estimates based on latest available census and survey data.

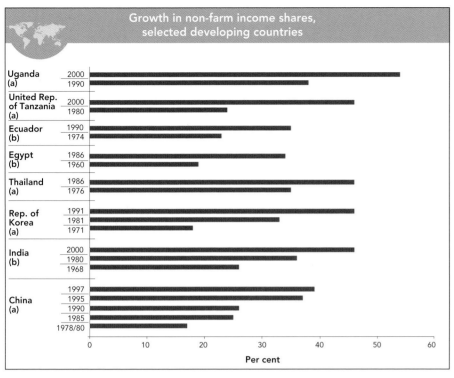

Source: Haggblade, Hazell and Reardon (2007).

Note: (a) Non-farm share of farm household income. (b) Non-farm share of rural income.

Non-farm income represents a significant and increasing share of rural income in developing countries

Non-farm income accounts for up to 42 per cent of rural household income, and non-farm employment up to one third of the rural labour force in the developing world. The non-farm share of household income is increasing over time. The sources of non-farm income are highly heterogeneous, including agro-processing, other manufacturing, trade and transport, construction, finance and personal services. Remittances account for a large share of non-farm income in some locations where mining is an important activity, as in Southern Africa.

The more dynamic the agricultural sector is, the more dynamic the rural non-farm sector tends to be due to strong linkages from agriculture to the rest of the rural economy. In settings characterized by a stagnant agricultural sector, rural households may be pushed to non-farm activities by lack of other opportunities.[19]

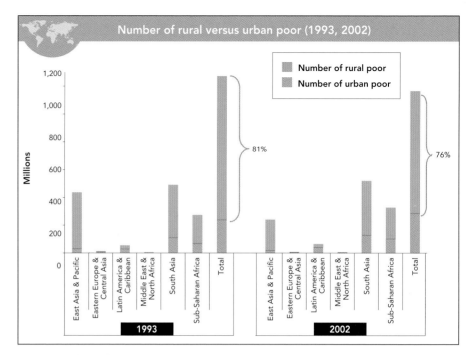

Source: Ravallion, Chen and Sangraula (2007).

Note: Data correspond to estimates of the urban-rural breakdown of absolute poverty measures (that is, using an international poverty line of 1 dollar a day) for the developing world, drawing on over 208 household surveys for 87 countries (representing 92 per cent of the population of the developing world), and exploiting the World Bank's Poverty Assessments for guidance on the urban-rural cost-of-living differential facing poor people, to supplement existing estimates of the purchasing-power-parity exchange rates for consumption.

Rural poverty rates have declined, but remain high in South Asia and in sub-Saharan Africa where the number of poor people has increased

The number of rural poor outweighs the number of urban poor by a large margin and poverty is still far more prevalent in rural areas. Policies to promote agricultural and rural development thus play a crucial role in poverty reduction. There are, however, important regional variations. In East Asia and the Pacific poverty is predominantly rural, whereas in Latin America and the Caribbean it is mostly urban.

The overall net poverty reduction observed in the 1993-2002 period is essentially due to a decrease of roughly 150 million in the number of rural poor. While this is partly due to rural-to-urban migration, the biggest factor has been a reduction in poverty within rural areas. In South Asia and sub-Saharan Africa, however, the absolute number of rural poor has increased over the period.[20]

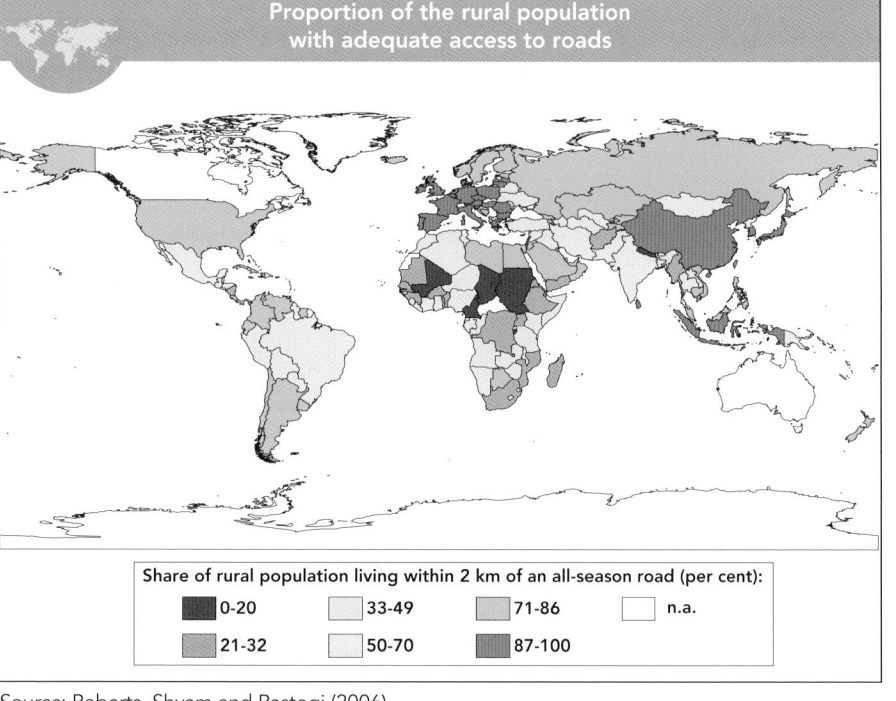

Proportion of the rural population with adequate access to roads

Share of rural population living within 2 km of an all-season road (per cent):

- 0-20
- 21-32
- 33-49
- 50-70
- 71-86
- 87-100
- n.a.

Source: Roberts, Shyam and Rastogi (2006).

A large proportion of the rural population in many developing countries is still excluded from the economic opportunities arising from access to decent roads

Road access rates are lowest in sub-Saharan Africa, but there are also some countries in Asia and Latin America where access is very poor.

Inadequate access to roads increases a variety of costs, from obtaining inputs to transporting goods to market to finding buyers and monitoring contracts. It can also lead to poor farm households' having to rely on private health care if transport costs to reach public health-care facilities are too high.

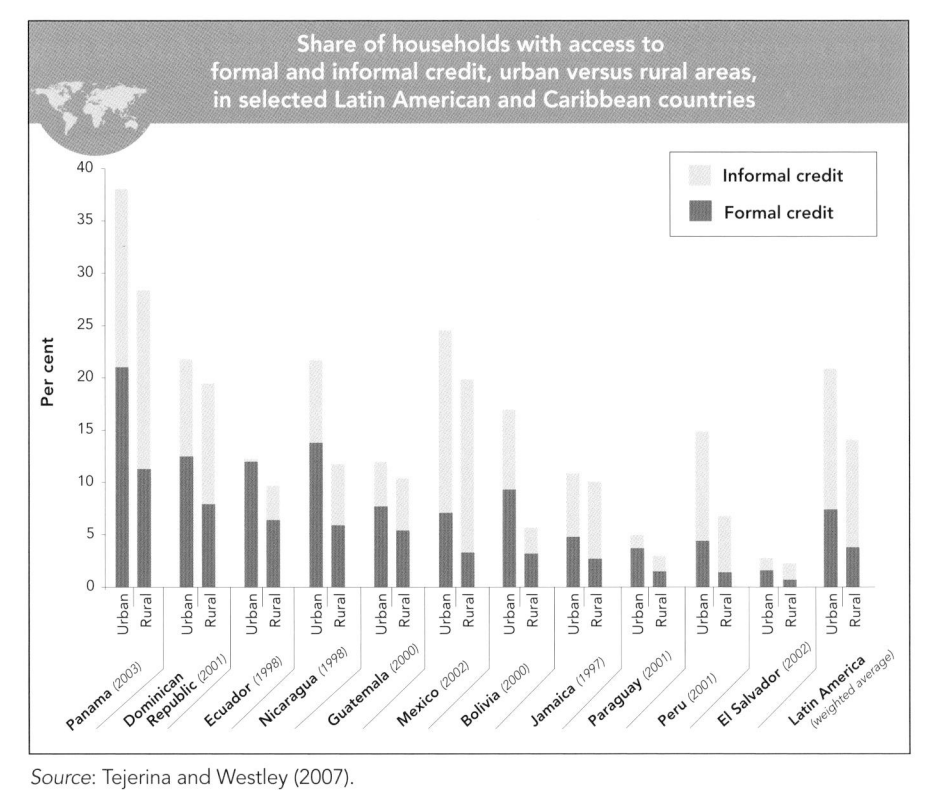

Share of households with access to formal and informal credit, urban versus rural areas, in selected Latin American and Caribbean countries

Legend:
- Informal credit
- Formal credit

Per cent (y-axis, 0 to 40)

Categories (Urban / Rural):
Panama (2003), Dominican Republic (2001), Ecuador (1998), Nicaragua (1998), Guatemala (2000), Mexico (2002), Bolivia (2000), Jamaica (1997), Paraguay (2001), Peru (2001), El Salvador (2002), Latin America (weighted average)

Source: Tejerina and Westley (2007).

Note: Date of most recent household survey year in parentheses.

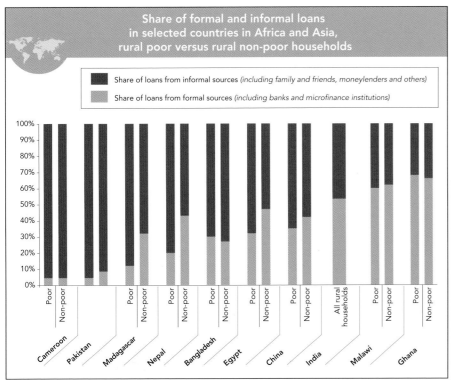

Share of formal and informal loans
in selected countries in Africa and Asia,
rural poor versus rural non-poor households

■ Share of loans from informal sources (including family and friends, moneylenders and others)

■ Share of loans from formal sources (including banks and microfinance institutions)

Countries (with Poor / Non-poor bars): Cameroon, Pakistan, Madagascar, Nepal, Bangladesh, Egypt, China, India, All rural households (Malawi), Malawi, Ghana

Source: Basu (2006) for India, and Zeller and Sharma (1998) for all other countries.

Rural households in developing countries are still largely reliant on informal sources for their finance needs

In several Latin American countries, access to formal credit is only half as common in rural areas as it is in urban areas.

Informal lenders provide the bulk of the loans to rural households in many countries. Their dominance as credit source is even greater among poor rural households. In Pakistan and Cameroon, for instance, less than 5 per cent of the amount borrowed by poor rural households was obtained from formal lenders, including banks and microfinance institutions.

In general, access to credit has a positive impact on household income, technology adoption and food consumption. These in turn have important long-term effects on household productivity and on poverty rates.[21]

A number of institutional and product innovations have been developed to address the specific needs of rural finance in developing countries, with varying degrees and forms of support from public policy (see map).

"Ensuring the rural poor have the necessary tools to build better lives for themselves and their children is a crucial step towards halving the proportion of people living in extreme poverty by 2015."

Innovative finance in rural areas

Mobile banking

In the Philippines, accredited rural banks are now permitted to offer electronically based financial services such as loan payments and collection of remittances. In Kenya, an innovative payment service (MPESA) allows customers without bank accounts to use their mobile phones to transfer money quickly, securely and across great distances, directly to another mobile phone user. [22]

Linking formal finance institutions to informal organizations

In India, a partnership between ICICI Bank, the country's second largest commercial bank, and a leading microfinance institution has been successful in linking the formal financial sector with poor microfinance clients. The approach is based on having microfinance institutions bear the responsibility of monitoring and recovering loans from individuals and self-help groups, while the commercial bank supplies credit and shares the risk. In Rwanda, CARE is helping mobilize the rural poor into village savings and credit associations and linking them to the existing network of credit unions in the country. [23]

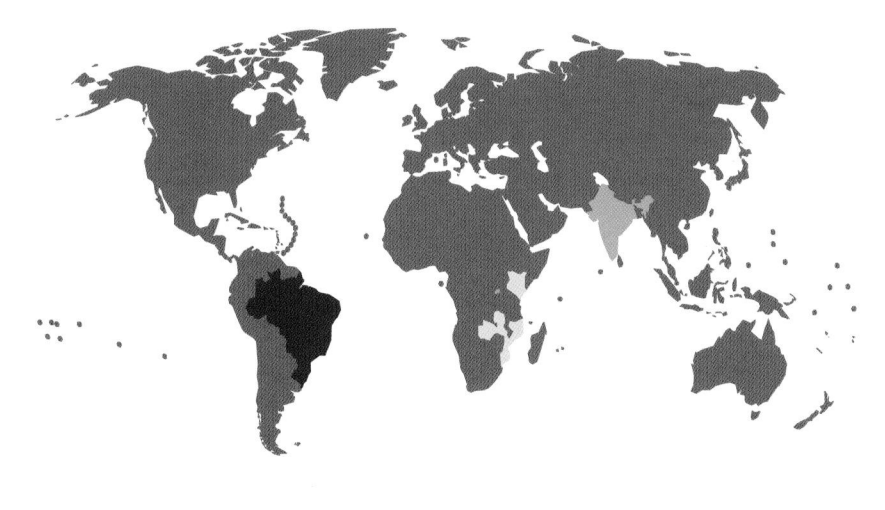

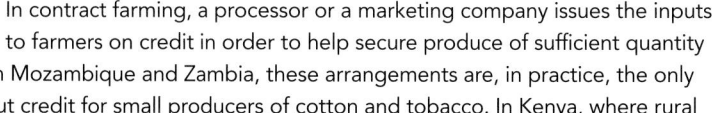

Contract farming as source of smallholder credit

In contract farming, a processor or a marketing company issues the inputs to farmers on credit in order to help secure produce of sufficient quantity and quality. In Mozambique and Zambia, these arrangements are, in practice, the only source of input credit for small producers of cotton and tobacco. In Kenya, where rural financial services are better developed, financing of inputs by processing and marketing companies is critical for the production of many high-value export crops, including tea, sugar and horticultural products. [24]

Weather-index-based insurance for agriculture

Weather-indexed risk management products represent an innovative alternative to the traditional crop insurance programmes for smallholder farmers in developing countries. Insurance pays out directly to farmers (India, Ukraine) or to Governments and/or humanitarian agencies that in turn support the affected farmers (Ethiopia, Malawi). Payments are linked to a weather proxy for crop losses like rainfall deficit, eliminating the need for monitoring actual losses. [25]

Correspondent banking

"Correspondents" are commercial entities whose primary business is other than the provision of financial services —typically retail outlets, including lottery kiosks, post offices—but which also offer such services in partnerships with banks. The current generation of correspondent banking arrangements is able to utilize technology to enhance the range, scale and quality of services provided. In Brazil, banks have recently developed extensive networks of such correspondents. As a result, all municipalities have access to financial services, including in poor remote regions. At the same time, such arrangements have resulted in lower costs and shared risks for participating financial institutions. [26]

Endnotes

18 World Bank (2007), *World Development Report 2008*.

19 S. Haggblade, P. Hazell and T. Reardon (2007), *Transforming the Rural Nonfarm Economy: Opportunities and Threats in the Developing World*, Johns Hopkins University Press, 512 p.

20 M. Ravallion, S. Chen and P. Sangraula (2007), "New evidence on the urbanization of global poverty", Policy Research Working Paper, No. 4199 (Washington, D.C.: World Bank).

21 P. Mosley (2001), "Microfinance and poverty in Bolivia", *The Journal of Development Studies*, vol. 37 (4), pp. 101-132; M. Zeller and M. Sharma (1998), *Rural Finance and Poverty Alleviation*, Food Policy Report, International Food Policy research Institute, Washington, D.C., June; and J. Yaron, P. B. McDonald, Jr., and G. L. Piprek (1997), *Rural Finance: Issues, Design and Best Practices*, Environmentally and Socially Sustainable Development Studies and Monographs Series 14, World Bank, Washington, D.C.

22 N. Hughes and S. Lonie (2007), "M-PESA: mobile money for the 'unbanked': turning cellphones into 24-hour tellers in Kenya", *Innovations: Technology, Governance, Globalization*, Winter/Spring 2007, 2 (1-2), pp. 63-81; and J. Owens (2007), "Leapfrogging access to finance with mobile phone technology: Philippine rural banks offering M-banking & M-commerce services", presentation, IFC/CGAP conference, "Next generation access to finance: gaining scale and reducing costs with technology and credit scoring", 17-19 September 2007, Washington, D.C., http://siteresources.worldbank.org/FSLP/Resources/JohnOwensshortversionupdated.pdf.

23 C. Aeschliman, F. Murekezi and J.-P. Ndoshoboye (2007), "Extending the outreach of Rwandan Peoples' Banks to the rural poor through village savings and credit associations", case study prepared for the Food and Agriculture Organization of the United Nations (FAO); and M. Harper (2005), "ICICI Bank and microfinance in India", case study prepared for the Food and Agriculture Organization of the United Nations (FAO).

24 IFAD (2003), "Agricultural marketing companies as sources of smallholder credit in Eastern and Southern Africa: experiences, insights and potential donor role", IFAD Rural Finance Case Studies, http://www.ifad.int/ruralfinance/policy/pf.pdf.

25 J. Syroka and E. Bryla (2007), "Developing index-based insurance for agriculture in developing countries", *Sustainable Development Innovation Briefs*, No. 2, March, http://www.un.org/esa/sustdev/publications/innovationbriefs/no2.pdf.

26 K. Anjali, K. Ajai Nair, A. Parsons and E. Urdapilleta (2006), "Expanding bank outreach through retail partnerships: correspondent banking in Brazil", World Bank Working Paper 85.

Sources for graphs and maps

United Nations, Department of Economic and Social Affairs (2006), *World Population Prospects: The 2006 Revision*, Population Division, http://esa.un.org/unpp.

United Nations, Department of Economic and Social Affairs (2005), *World Urbanization Prospects: The 2005 Revision*, Population Division, http://esa.un.org/unpp.

S. Haggblade, P. Hazell and T. Reardon (2007), *Transforming the Rural Nonfarm Economy: Opportunities and Threats in the Developing World*, Johns Hopkins University Press, 512 p.

M. Ravallion, S. Chen and P. Sangraula (2007), "New evidence on the urbanization of global poverty", Policy Research Working Paper No. 4199 (Washington, D.C.: World Bank).

P. Roberts, K. C. Shyam and C. Rastogi (2006), "Rural Access Index: a key development indicator", The World Bank Group, Transport Papers, TP10, 49 p.

L. Tejerina and G. D. Westley (2007), "Financial services for the poor: household survey sources and gaps in borrowing and saving", Sustainable Development Department Technical Papers Series, Inter-American Development Bank.

P. Basu (2006), *Improving Access to Finance for India's Rural Poor*, Directions in Development, World Bank, Washington, D.C.

M. Zeller and M. Sharma (1998), *Rural Finance and Poverty Alleviation*, Food Policy Report, International Food Policy Research Institute, Washington, D.C., June.

Sources for quotes

Statement of Lennart Båge, President of IFAD (2007), high-level meeting of the heads of the coordination group institutions and the international donors and development institutions, http://www.ifad.org/events/op/2007/kuwait.htm.

IFAD, "Investing in microfinance: microfinance and the Millennium Development Goals", http://www.ifad.org/events/yom/mdgs.htm.

LAND

Access to and distribution of agricultural land

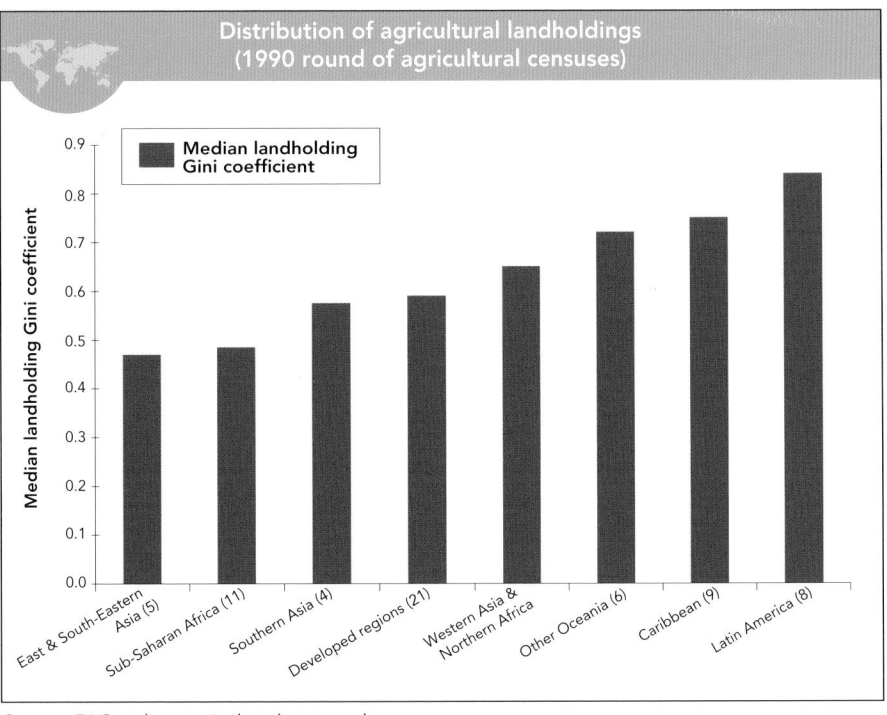

Distribution of agricultural landholdings (1990 round of agricultural censuses)

Median landholding Gini coefficient

Median landholding Gini coefficient (y-axis: 0.0 to 0.9)

- East & South-Eastern Asia (5)
- Sub-Saharan Africa (11)
- Southern Asia (4)
- Developed regions (21)
- Western Asia & Northern Africa
- Other Oceania (6)
- Caribbean (9)
- Latin America (8)

Source: FAO online agricultural census data.

Note: The numbers in parentheses indicate the number of countries from which medians were obtained. FAO defines an agricultural holding as an economic unit of agricultural production under single management comprising all livestock kept and all land used wholly or partly for agricultural production purposes, without regard to title, legal form, or size.

Land distribution remains highly unequal in some regions

The Gini coefficient measures inequality or concentration in a distribution, in this case of land. It is defined as a ratio with values between 0 and 1, where 0 corresponds to perfect equality and 1 to perfect inequality.

Latin American countries tend to have higher inequality in agricultural land distribution than other regions. The low median value for sub-Saharan African countries suggests that low land inequality per se does not lead to high agricultural productivity. If, however, Africa were to experience an agricultural technology revolution, the benefits could be widely shared.

When other influences on land productivity are accounted for, the degree of land inequality is found to be negatively related to agricultural land productivity at the macrolevel. This suggests that the distribution of land within countries is not optimal and land markets are not functioning properly.[27]

Beyond agricultural productivity, land inequality has been shown to have a negative impact on other key aspects of economic development—education, institutions and financial development—and on poverty.[28]

Land as a resource base

Land degradation in all its forms is a threat to food production and rural livelihoods, especially in the poorest areas of the developing world. Existing estimates of the current global extent and severity of land degradation should be considered indicative at best. According to the 1991 Global Land Assessment of Degradation (GLASOD), based on expert opinion, nearly 2 billion hectares worldwide (22 per cent of all cropland, pasture, forest, and woodland) have been degraded since the 1950s. Africa and Latin America appear to have the highest proportion of degraded agricultural land, and Asia has the highest proportion of degraded forest land.[29]

Nevertheless, much agricultural production is sustainable, and in some cases large areas have been under continuous cultivation for centuries, if not millennia. Some land degradation in rural areas has little to do with agriculture. Logging, mining and tourism also degrade land through deforestation, conversion of natural ecosystems, and pollution.[30]

Productivity growth of high-input agriculture has slowed down

Most of the increase in agricultural production over the last four decades can be attributed to "Green Revolution" technologies—including high-yielding cultivars, chemical fertilizers and pesticides, and irrigation—and mechanization. Global fertilizer consumption increased from 23 kilograms per hectare of cropland in 1961 to 92 kg per hectare in 2002, and the share of global irrigated land increased from 12 to 19 per cent over the same period.[31]

Yield growth has slowed down, and modern inputs have caused environmental damage in many regions, including degradation of water quality due to chemical pollution, salinization due to irrigation, and loss of biodiversity as a result of habitat destruction, including of pollinators that are critical to agricultural production. Many insect pests and some weeds have evolved pesticide resistance, while promotion of high-yielding cultivars and livestock breeds has substantially reduced agrobiodiversity, increasing vulnerability to pests and diseases (e.g., in Sri Lanka, the number of rice varieties decreased from 2,000 in the 1950s to fewer than 100 today).[32]

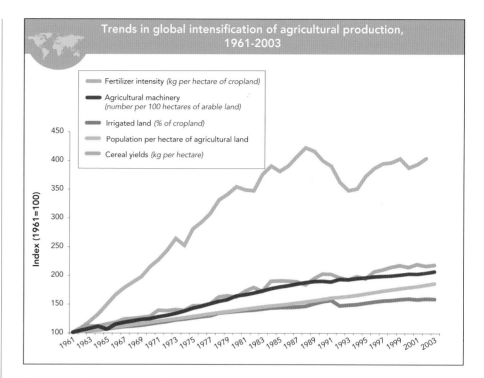

Trends in global intensification of agricultural production, 1961-2003

Legend:
- Fertilizer intensity (kg per hectare of cropland)
- Agricultural machinery (number per 100 hectares of arable land)
- Irrigated land (% of cropland)
- Population per hectare of agricultural land
- Cereal yields (kg per hectare)

Index (1961=100)

Source: World Bank (2007) and FAOSTAT archives.

Note: Agricultural machinery refers to the number of wheel and crawler tractors (excluding garden tractors).

> " Changes in land cover, driven by the way people use land, are perhaps the most important single change in terrestrial ecosystems . . . "

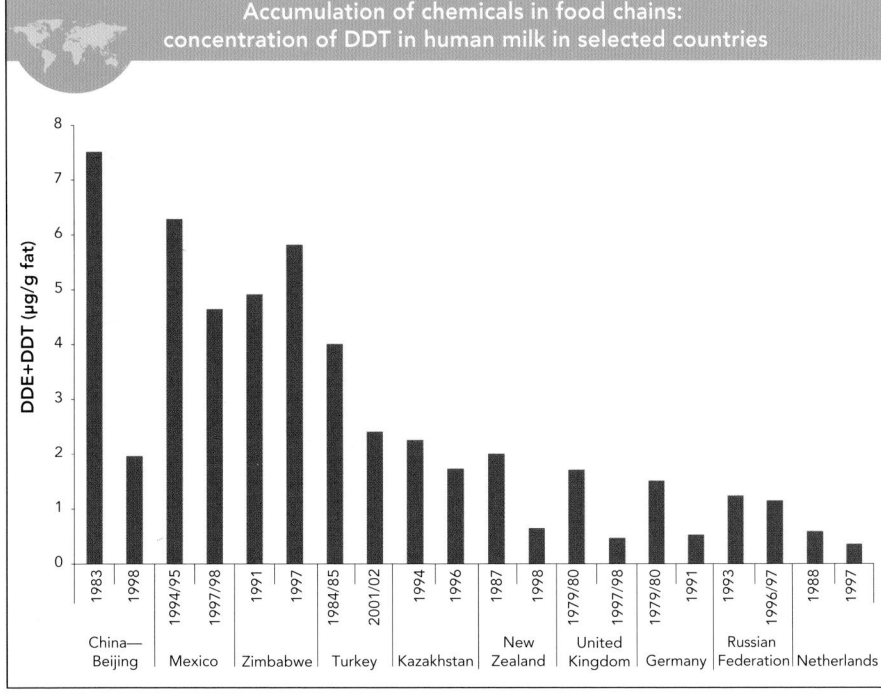

Accumulation of chemicals in food chains: concentration of DDT in human milk in selected countries

DDE+DDT (µg/g fat)

China—Beijing: 1983, 1998
Mexico: 1994/95, 1997/98
Zimbabwe: 1991, 1997
Turkey: 1984/85, 2001/02
Kazakhstan: 1994, 1996
New Zealand: 1987, 1998
United Kingdom: 1979/80, 1997/98
Germany: 1979/80, 1991
Russian Federation: 1993, 1996/97
Netherlands: 1988, 1997

Source: Wong and others (2005).

Note: Human milk is considered to be a reliable means for measuring human exposure to the fat-soluble POPs, including POP pesticides.

Increased awareness regarding the detrimental effects of DDT has led to its elimination in many countries

Some pesticides accumulate in food chains and surface waters for long periods. The 2001 Stockholm Convention on Persistent Organic Pollutants (POPs) seeks the elimination or restriction of production and use of all intentionally produced POPs, but some remain popular as agrochemicals in developing countries, and DDT use for malaria control is allowed under the Convention and is still widespread in poor countries like Zimbabwe. Globally, the decline in DDT levels in the human population is the result of lower utilization following its ban as an agrochemical in many countries. The total usage of DDT in European countries decreased from some 28,000 tons in 1970 to zero in 1996. In Mexico, DDT use has been restricted since 1990. In China, the ban on DDT production and agricultural use was enforced in 1983.[33]

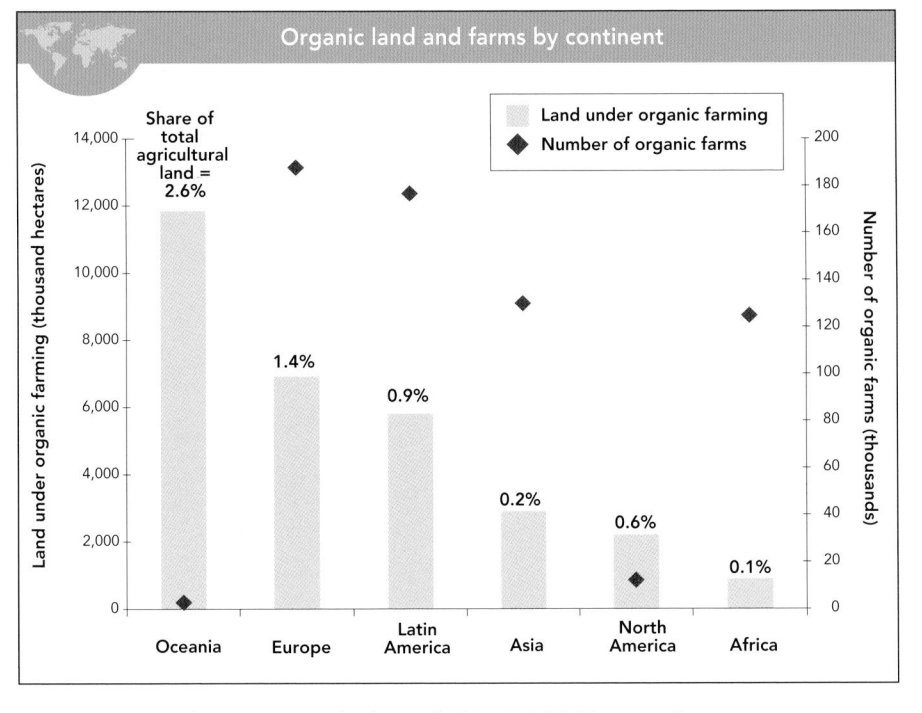

Organic land and farms by continent

Land under organic farming (thousand hectares)
Number of organic farms (thousands)

Legend: Land under organic farming; Number of organic farms

Oceania: Share of total agricultural land = 2.6%
Europe: 1.4%
Latin America: 0.9%
Asia: 0.2%
North America: 0.6%
Africa: 0.1%

Source: IFOAM and FiBL (2007) on the basis of SOEL-FiBL (2007) survey data.

Note: Land under certified organic farming obtained from data published by agricultural ministries and/or as declared by surveyed organizations (e.g., national and international certification bodies). Survey results cover 63 per cent of all countries. Agricultural land includes cropland and permanent pastures.

Land under organic farming is increasing but remains concentrated in a few countries

Almost 31 million hectares are currently managed under organic farming methods by over 600,000 farmers worldwide, or roughly 1 per cent of agricultural land. The region with the most land under organic cultivation is Oceania (basically on account of Australia), followed by Europe (mostly in the EU) and Latin America (mostly in Argentina, Brazil and Uruguay). In terms of number of farms, however, the distribution is slightly different. Most organic farms are located in Europe, followed by Latin America, but Africa and Asia represent one fourth of the total each.[34]

Organic agriculture has a smaller adverse impact on the natural resource base, ecosystems and the health of agricultural workers than conventional agriculture. In addition, it offers export opportunities for developing countries, which in many cases have a comparative advantage due to relatively abundant labour supply and low use of agrochemicals. Still, significant challenges face the poorest countries in entering export markets because of the small volumes traded and the substantial investments required in developing certification bodies and securing recognition for that certification in developed country markets.[35]

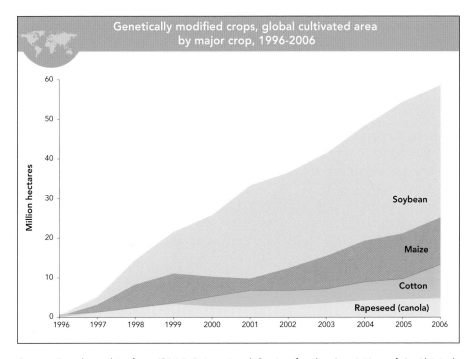

Genetically modified crops, global cultivated area by major crop, 1996-2006

Source: Based on data from ISAAA (International Service for the Acquisition of Agri-biotech Applications).

Over the past decade, genetically modified (GM) crops have been adopted rapidly at the global level

In the developing world, adoption remains limited to a number of middle-income countries. The most widely used GM technologies involve herbicide tolerance (HT) applied in soybean and canola, and insect resistance (IR) applied in maize and cotton. However, the suitability of GM crops remains controversial, both in terms of economic benefits for developing countries and in terms of long-term environmental impact (e.g., from reduced agro-biodiversity and from increased herbicide use).

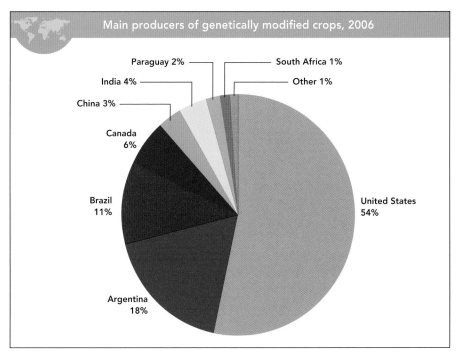

Main producers of genetically modified crops, 2006

Source: Based on data from ISAAA (International Service for the Acquisition of Agri-biotech Applications).

Economic returns to adoption of genetically modified crops in developing countries are highly variable. Locally adapted transgenic cotton varieties in China, for instance, compete directly with imported, patent-protected varieties, reducing the seed price for farmers. In Argentina, on the other hand, farmers have to pay significantly higher prices for IR cotton seeds, and as a result adoption rates have been low. In contrast, Argentina is among the largest producers of herbicide-tolerant soybeans, which are not patented locally.[36]

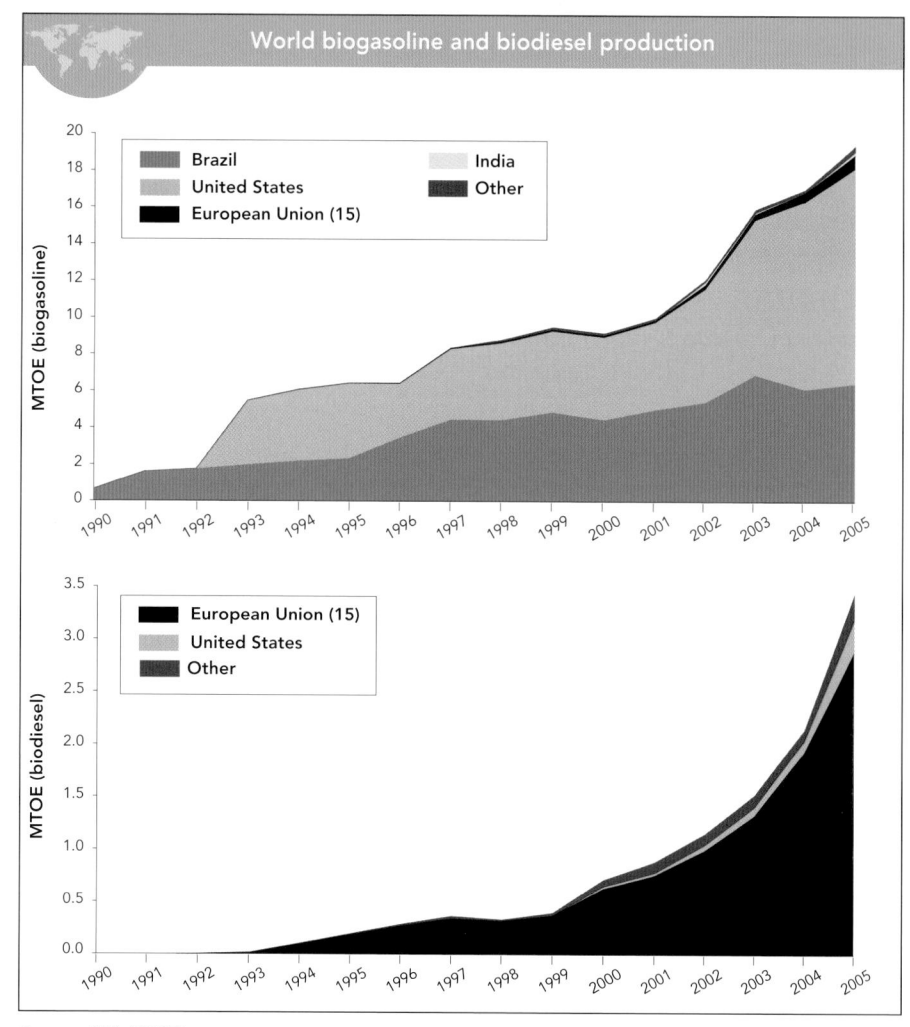

World biogasoline and biodiesel production

Legend (top chart):
- Brazil
- United States
- European Union (15)
- India
- Other

MTOE (biogasoline)

Legend (bottom chart):
- European Union (15)
- United States
- Other

MTOE (biodiesel)

Source: IEA (2007).

Production of crops for biofuels has increased sharply since the beginning of the 1990s

The agricultural sector can contribute to mitigating GHG emissions through the production of biofuels, although net effects are highly dependent on the type of feedstock used, methods of cultivation and conversion technologies, and full life-cycle emissions from farm to fuel tank.

Subsidies for biofuel crop production and regulations mandating increasing levels of biofuels in road-transport fuel mixes are being put in place, while barriers to cheaper imports through tariffs and discriminatory domestic taxes are restricting access of developing countries—some of which are highly competitive in biofuel production—to several major OECD markets.[37]

Expanded biofuels production can have serious local environmental impacts, including degradation of soils and deforestation. Also, biofuel production is already pushing up certain food crop prices.[38]

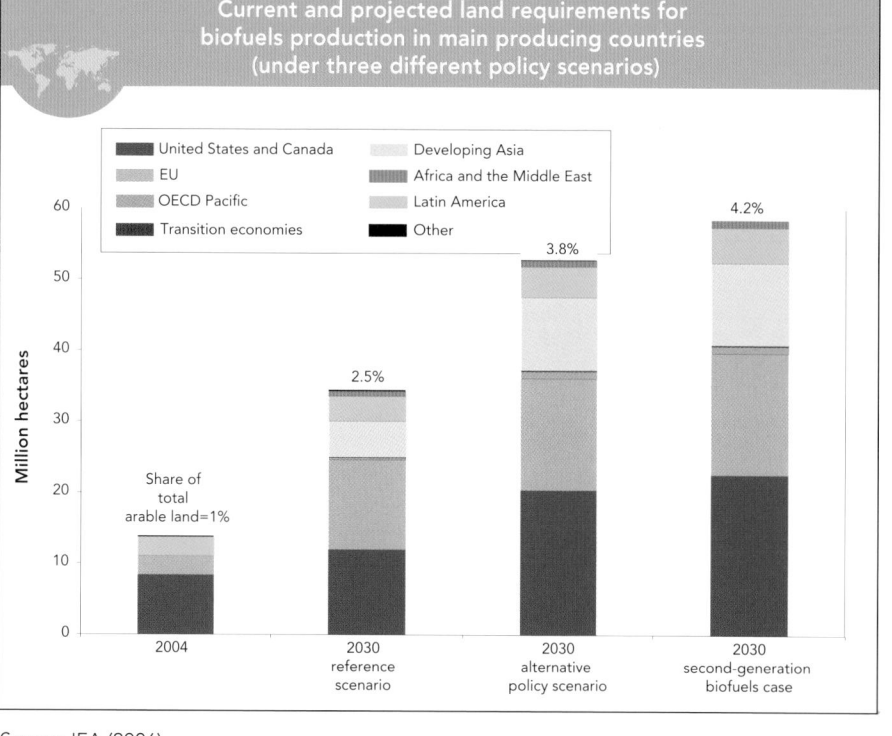

Current and projected land requirements for biofuels production in main producing countries (under three different policy scenarios)

Legend:
- United States and Canada
- EU
- OECD Pacific
- Transition economies
- Developing Asia
- Africa and the Middle East
- Latin America
- Other

Million hectares

Share of total arable land=1%

- 2004
- 2030 reference scenario — 2.5%
- 2030 alternative policy scenario — 3.8%
- 2030 second-generation biofuels case — 4.2%

Source: IEA (2006).

Note: Alternative policy scenario includes policies currently under consideration around the world to promote production and use of biofuels; second-generation biofuels case assumes large-scale introduction of ligno-cellulosic technologies, raising biofuels share in transport demand to 10 per cent globally by 2030.

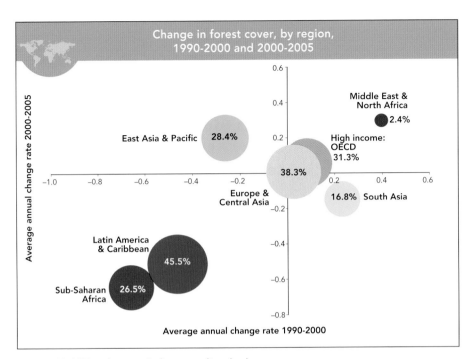

Change in forest cover, by region, 1990-2000 and 2000-2005

Average annual change rate 2000-2005 (vertical axis, 0.6 to -0.8)
Average annual change rate 1990-2000 (horizontal axis, -1.0 to 0.6)

Middle East & North Africa 2.4%
East Asia & Pacific 28.4%
High income: OECD 31.3%
Europe & Central Asia 38.3%
16.8% South Asia
Latin America & Caribbean 45.5%
Sub-Saharan Africa 26.5%

Source: World Development Indicators online database.

Note: Size of bubbles corresponds to forest area as a percentage of total land area. Forest area is land under natural or planted stands of trees.

Global forest cover continues to experience a net decline

Between 1990 and 2005, global forest cover decreased by approximately 1.3 million square kilometres, a 0.2 per cent average annual loss, with the largest absolute net losses taking place in Indonesia and Brazil. There are, however, substantial differences between regions, and between the first decade of that period and the last five years. The highest rates of net loss in forest cover are found in sub-Saharan Africa and in Latin America and the Caribbean, which was the region with the largest share of forested area in the world in 2005. In sub-Saharan Africa, although the rate of loss declined slightly in recent years, there are only a few countries in which forest cover is increasing.[39]

In East Asia and the Pacific, there has been a recovery in forested area in the 2000-2005 period, mainly as a result of the substantial increase in forest cover in China. The net increase at the regional level is built mainly on large investments in forest plantations in several countries, while natural forest area continues to decline.[40]

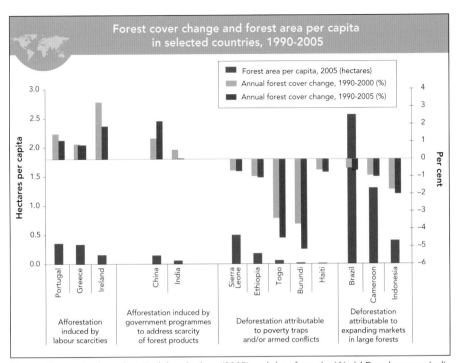

Forest cover change and forest area per capita in selected countries, 1990-2005

Legend:
- Forest area per capita, 2005 (hectares)
- Annual forest cover change, 1990-2000 (%)
- Annual forest cover change, 1990-2005 (%)

Hectares per capita (left axis, 0.0 to 3.0)
Per cent (right axis, -6 to 4)

Countries: Portugal, Greece, Ireland | China, India | Sierra Leone, Ethiopia, Togo, Burundi, Haiti | Brazil, Cameroon, Indonesia

Categories:
- Afforestation induced by labour scarcities
- Afforestation induced by government programmes to address scarcity of forest products
- Deforestation attributable to poverty traps and/or armed conflicts
- Deforestation attributable to expanding markets in large forests

Source: Categories based on Rudel and others (2005) and data from the World Development Indicators online database.

Trajectories of forest cover change vary widely

Over the past 15 years, forest cover has expanded in two groups of countries—those where rural labour shortages due to growth in non-farm employment and rural-to-urban migration have caused some lands to be converted back from farms (e.g., in Europe) and those where government programmes have strongly promoted afforestation in response to timber product shortages and serious flooding due in part to deforestation (e.g., China and India).[41] The Chinese Government's Upland Conversion Programme has resulted in extensive tree plantations.

Meanwhile, another two groups have seen significant forest area decline—poor, land-scarce countries (e.g., Togo, Burundi and Haiti) and countries with large per capita forest endowments and profitable forestry industries (e.g., Brazil, Cameroon and Indonesia). In the first group, farmers without access to technology, capital or markets could not improve land productivity and hence expanded the area under cultivation. In the latter, secondary forests and plantations have increased, but only partially offset the decline in old-growth forests.[42]

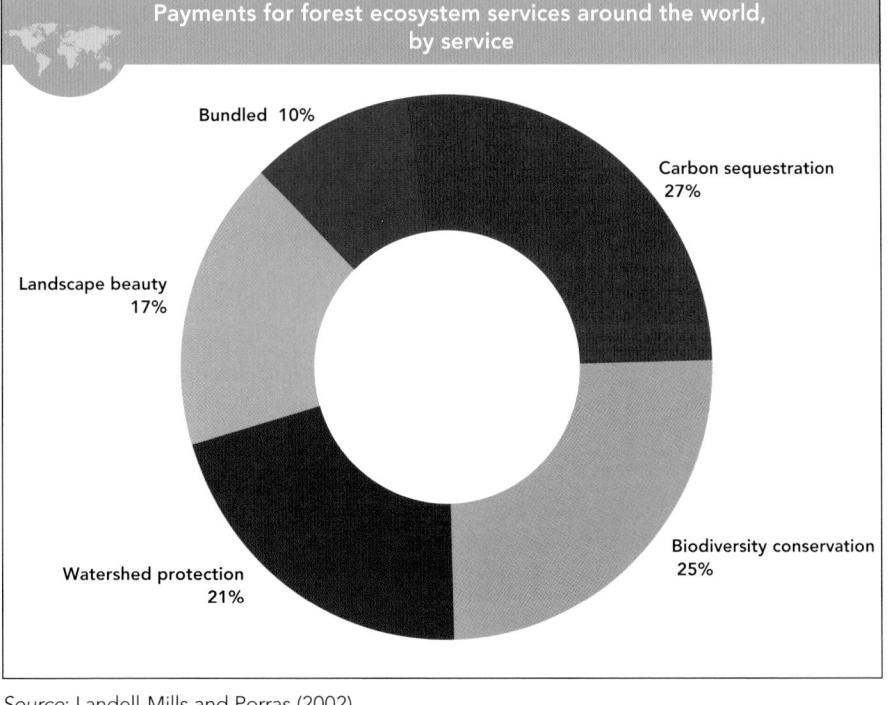

Payments for forest ecosystem services around the world, by service

- Bundled 10%
- Carbon sequestration 27%
- Landscape beauty 17%
- Watershed protection 21%
- Biodiversity conservation 25%

Source: Landell-Mills and Porras (2002).

Note: The breakdown is based on a total of 287 cases.

The use of innovative instruments to address deforestation and its root causes is increasing

The decline in forest area calls for revising widely held views on conservation and land-use policy. New research suggests that reserve areas established for indigenous peoples are as effective as uninhabited nature parks in preventing burning and clear-cutting.[43]

Innovative instruments, such as payments for ecosystem services, are being more widely used to conserve forests, recognizing their watershed, biodiversity and carbon sequestration value. Payments may come from downstream users of those services, conservation groups, tourists, governments or others. Payments for forest conservation have started to be used in the State of Amazonas in Brazil as one measure in the package under its 2007 Climate Change Law.[44]

> **Land degradation control has major global benefits . . . as the vehicle to a future with conservation of biodiversity, control of climate change and prevention of land degradation simultaneously achieved.**

Endnotes

27 D. Vollrath (2007), "Land distribution and international agricultural productivity", *American Journal of Agricultural Economics*, 89(1), pp. 202-216.

28 L. A. Erickson and D. Vollrath (2007), "Land distribution and financial system development", IMF Working Paper, No. 07/83, April.

29 S. J. Scherr and S. Yadav (2001), "Land degradation in the developing world—issues and policy options for 2020", chapter 21 in *The Unfinished Agenda: Perspectives on Overcoming Hunger, Poverty, and Environmental Degradation*, P. Pinstrup-Andersen and R. Pandya-Lorch, eds., IFPRI, 302 p.

30 World Bank (2007), *World Development Report 2008*.

31 J. A. Foley and others (2005), "Global consequences of land use", *Science*, 309, pp. 570-574.

32 L. A. Thrupp (2000), "Linking agricultural biodiversity and food security: the valuable role of agrobiodiversity for sustainable agriculture", *International Affairs*, 76(2), pp. 265-281.

33 M. H. Wong, A. O. W. Leung, J. K. Y. Chan and M. P. K. Choi (2005), "A review on the usage of POP pesticides in China, with emphasis on DDT loadings in human milk", *Chemosphere*, 60(6), pp. 740-752.

34 International Federation of Organic Agriculture (IFOAM) and Research Institute of Organic Agriculture (FiBL) (2007), *The World of Organic Agriculture: Statistics & Emerging Trends 2007*, Germany, 196 p.

35 M. A. Altieri, P. Rosset and L. A. Thrupp (2001), "The potential of agroecology to combat hunger in the developing world", chapter 19 in *The Unfinished Agenda: Perspectives on Overcoming Hunger, Poverty, and Environmental Degradation*, P. Pinstrup-Andersen and R. Pandya-Lorch, eds., IFPRI, 302 p.

36 T. Raney (2006), "Economic impact of transgenic crops in developing countries", *Current Opinion in Biotechnology*, 17, pp. 1-5.

37 R. Steenblik (2007), Government support for ethanol and biodiesel in selected OECD countries—a synthesis of reports addressing subsidies for biofuels in Australia, Canada, the European Union, Switzerland and the United States, Global Subsidies Initiative, IISD, http://www.globalsubsidies.org/IMG/pdf/biofuel_synthesis_report_26_9_07_master_2_.pdf.

38 UN-Energy (2007), Sustainable bioenergy: a framework for decision-makers, http://esa.un.org/un-energy/pdf/susdev.Biofuels.FAO.pdf.

39 FAO (2007), *The State of the World's Forests 2007*.

40 FAO (2007), *The State of the World's Forests 2007*.

41 T. K. Rudel, O. T. Coomes, E. Moran, F. Achard, A. Angelsen, J. Xu and E. Lambin (2005), "Forest transitions: towards a global understanding of land use change", *Global Environmental Change*, Part A, 15(1), pp. 23-31.

42 T. K. Rudel, O. T. Coomes, E. Moran, F. Achard, A. Angelsen, J. Xu and E. Lambin (2005), "Forest transitions: towards a global understanding of land use change", *Global Environmental Change*, Part A, 15(1), pp. 23-31.

43 D. Nepstad, S. Schwartzman, B. Bamberger, M. Santilli, D. Ray, P. Schlesinger, P. Lefebvre, A. Alencar, E. Prinz, G. Fiske and A. Rolla (2006), "Inhibition of Amazon deforestation and fire by parks and indigenous lands", *Conservation Biology*, 20 (1), pp. 65-73; and J. C. Paulo Oliveira, G. P. Asner, D. E. Knapp, Angélica Almeyda, Ricardo Galván-Gildemeister, Sam Keene, Rebecca F. Raybin and Richard C. Smith (2007), "Land-use allocation protects the Peruvian Amazon", *Science*, vol. 317 (5842).

44 FAO (2007), *The State of Food and Agriculture: Paying Farmers for Environmental Services*; and The Katoomba Group (2004), Conservation backgrounder, http://ecosystemmarketplace.com/pages/static/about.conservation_backgrounder.php.

Sources for graphs and maps

FAO online agricultural census data, http://www.fao.org/es/ess/census/default.asp.

World Bank (2007), *World Development Indicators 2007*.

FAOSTAT archives, http://faostat.fao.org.

M. H. Wong, A. O. W. Leung, J. K. Y. Chan and M. P. K. Choi (2005), "A review on the usage of POP pesticides in China, with emphasis on DDT loadings in human milk", *Chemosphere*, 60(6), pp. 740-752.

International Federation of Organic Agriculture (IFOAM) and Research Institute of Organic Agriculture (FiBL) (2007), *The World of Organic Agriculture: Statistics & Emerging Trends 2007*, Germany, 196 pp.

Foundation Ecology and Agriculture (SOEL) and Research Institute of Organic Agriculture (FiBL) (2007), Global survey on organic farming.

International Service for the Acquisition of Agri-biotech Applications, http://www.isaaa.org.

IEA (2007), Renewables Information—Primary Energy Supply, Transformation and Final Consumption of Renewable Products (TJ) Vol. 2007 release 01 (Organisation for Economic Co-operation and Development).

IEA (2006), *World Energy Outlook 2006*.

World Development Indicators online database, http://devdata.worldbank.org/dataonline.

T. K. Rudel, O. T. Coomes, E. Moran, F. Achard, A. Angelsen, J. Xu and E. Lambin (2005), "Forest transitions: towards a global understanding of land use change", *Global Environmental Change*, Part A, 15(1), pp. 23-31.

World Development Indicators online database, http://devdata.worldbank.org/dataonline.

N. Landell-Mills and I. T. Porras (2002), "Silver bullet or fools' gold? A global review of markets for forest environmental services and their impact on the poor", Instruments for Sustainable Private Sector Forestry Series, London, International Institute for Environment and Development.

Sources for quotes

Millennium Ecosystem Assessment (2005), *Ecosystems and Human Well-being: Current State and Trends*, p. 829.

G. Gísladóttir and M. Stocking (2005), "Land degradation control and its global environmental benefits", *Land Degradation and Development*, vol. 16 (2), pp. 99-112.

DESERTIFICATION

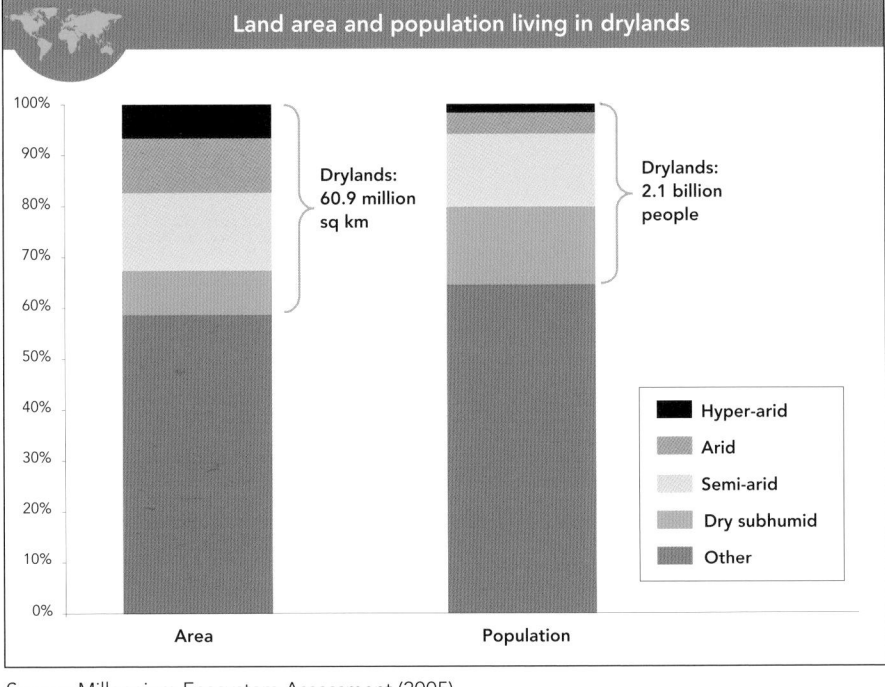

Land area and population living in drylands

Drylands:
60.9 million
sq km

Drylands:
2.1 billion
people

- ■ Hyper-arid
- ▨ Arid
- ▢ Semi-arid
- ▨ Dry subhumid
- ▨ Other

Area

Population

Source: Millennium Ecosystem Assessment (2005).

Note: Drylands are defined as areas with an aridity index value of less than 0.65, that is, areas in which annual mean potential evapotranspiration is at least 1.5 times greater than annual mean precipitation.

Drylands cover roughly 40 per cent of the earth's land surface and are inhabited by over 2 billion people, approximately one third of the world's population

About 90 per cent live in developing countries. A large share of the dryland population depends on crop and livestock production for their livelihoods. Whereas most area in drylands consists of rangeland (65 per cent), one fourth of it is able to sustain cultivation, although with productivity constraints from low soil moisture. Dryland rangelands support half of the world's livestock and provide forage for wildlife.[45]

“The impact of desertification is intensifying due to climate change, which is reducing the availability of freshwater, fertile soil, and forest and vegetation. As the degraded land loses value, investments in agriculture and rural development decline even more.”

—Ban Ki-moon
United Nations Secretary-General

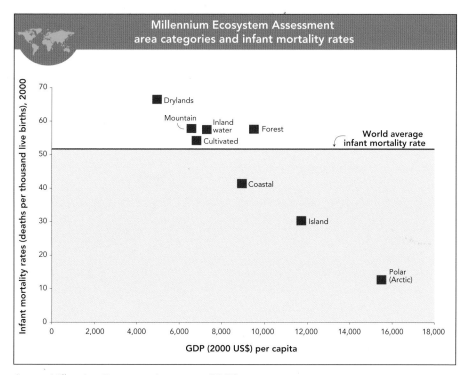

Millennium Ecosystem Assessment area categories and infant mortality rates

Source: Millennium Ecosystem Assessment (2005).

Note: The Millennium Ecosystem Assessment used 10 categories of systems to report its global findings. Ecosystems in each category share a suite of biological, climatic and social factors that tend to differ across categories. These categories are, however, not ecosystems themselves. Each contains a number of ecosystems and they overlap. Urban systems are excluded.

Drylands have the lowest GDP per capita and the highest infant mortality rates

At a global level, there are only a limited number of measures of human well-being available through which to assess patterns across ecosystem boundaries. Population, infant mortality rates and GDP can be obtained using data from subnational sources. The figure shows that drylands have the lowest GDP per capita and the highest infant mortality rates. This does not imply causality. Still, the high incidence of poverty combined with heavy dependence on fragile ecosystems for livelihoods makes dryland populations especially vulnerable to further land degradation and declines in ecosystem services.[46]

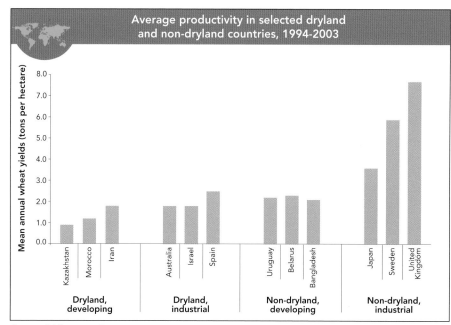

Average productivity in selected dryland and non-dryland countries, 1994-2003

Source: Millennium Ecosystem Assessment (2005).

There is a relative advantage of cultivation in non-dryland countries, but agroecological differences are only one part of the story

Yield differentials between developing dryland countries and developed dryland countries are modest, suggesting that nature may be the binding constraint. In the case of non-dryland wheat, by contrast, the yield differentials between developing countries and industrial countries are very wide. Moreover, industrialized dryland countries exhibit wheat yields nearly as high as those produced by non-dryland developing countries. Thus, socio-economic, institutional and technological conditions also matter.[47]

> ❝ Combating desertification yields multiple local and global benefits and helps mitigate biodiversity loss and human-induced global climate change. ❞

A. Percentage change in vegetation greenness in the Sahel, 1982-2003

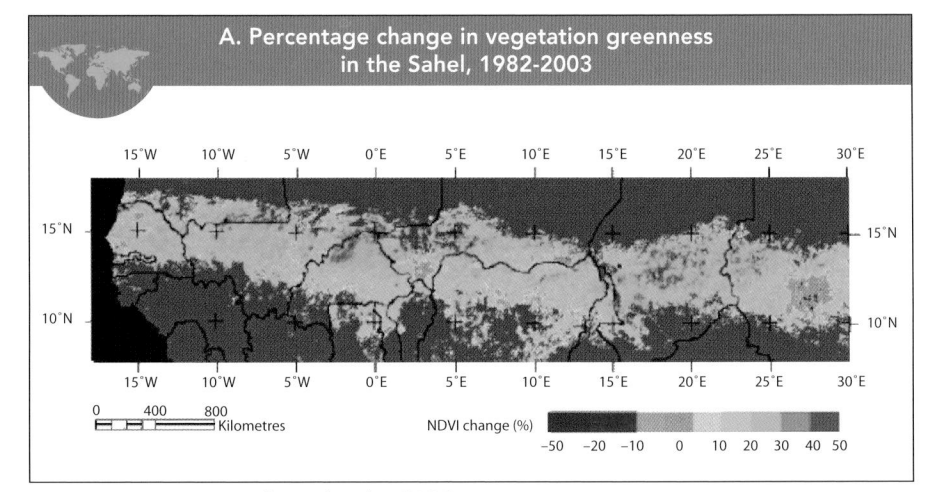

Kilometres

NDVI change (%)
−50 −20 −10 0 10 20 30 40 50

Source: Herrmann, Anyamba and Tucker (2005).

Note: Overall trends in vegetation greenness throughout the period 1982-2003 based on monthly Advanced Very High Resolution Radiometer, Normalized Difference Vegetation Index (AVHRR NDVI) time series. Percentages express changes in average NDVI between 1982 and 2003.

B. Effect of rainfall on vegetation greenness

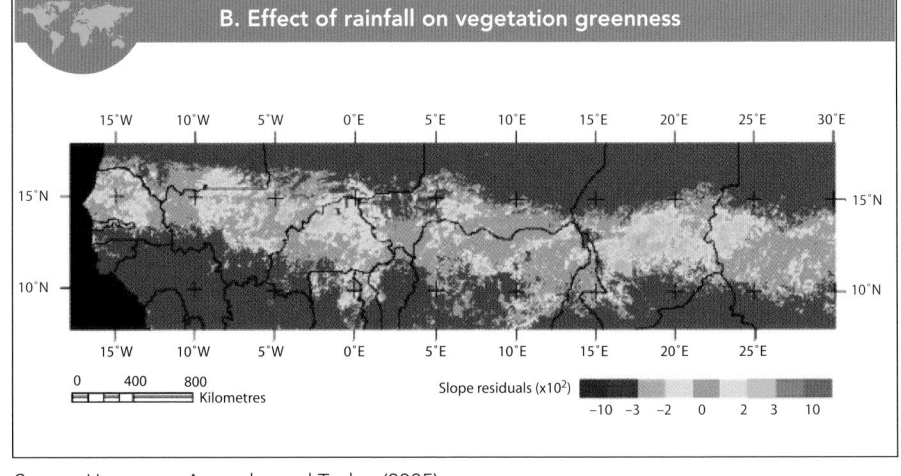

Kilometres

Slope residuals (x10²)
−10 −3 −2 0 2 3 10

Source: Herrmann, Anyamba and Tucker (2005).

Note: Overall trends in the residual NDVI throughout the period 1982-2003 based on regression of vegetation greenness (AVHRR NDVI) on 3-monthly cumulative rainfall. Slopes of residual NDVI trend lines between 1982 and 2003 are expressed in units of NDVI x 10^4.

Land-cover recovery in south-western Niger (Galma village)

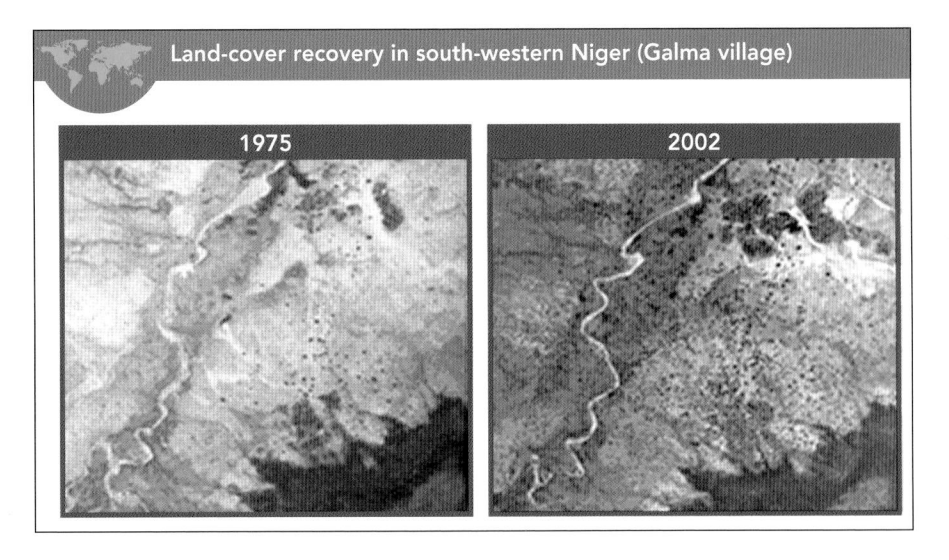

Source: G. Tappan, USGS Data Center for EROS, South Dakota.

Note: The black spots are mature trees. The aerial photo on the left shows that there were very few trees in the village of Galma in 1975. The satellite image on the right shows not only that the village has increased in size, but that there are also many more trees.

Innovations building on indigenous knowledge have helped reverse desertification processes in some parts of the world

In the Sahel, the most recent analyses indicate that there has been a greening of most of the region since the early 1990s. Figure A shows that, for the period 1982-2003, the overall trend in vegetation greenness is positive over a large portion of the Sahel region, reaching up to 50 per cent increase in parts of Mali, Mauritania and Chad, and confirming previous findings at a regional scale. The spatial pattern of the effect of rainfall on vegetation greenness in figure B further reveals that, although there are large areas in which changes in vegetation greenness correspond closely to what is expected from variations in rainfall (grey areas), there are also regions where the vegetation has been greening more than can be explained by rainfall alone (green areas). These "positive hot spots" are concentrated in parts of Senegal, Mauritania, Mali, the Niger, the Central Plateau of Burkina Faso and large portions of Chad. In some cases (e.g., Niger Delta of Mali; south-western Mauritania), this can be explained by an expansion of irrigation. In other areas, however, a recovery of vegetation greenness beyond what would be expected from the recovery of rainfall can be attributed to increased investment and improvements in soil and water conservation techniques building on traditional knowledge (e.g., Central Plateau of Burkina Faso, Tahoua and Maradi regions in the Niger).[48]

In northern Nigeria and the Sudan, vegetation greening has fallen short of what would be expected from the increase in rainfall. This has been particularly sharp in northern Nigeria. One explanation is the neglect of good land-use practices.[49]

Irrigation and land degradation in drylands: the Aral Sea

1989 | 2003

Source: NASA Earth Observatory.

Paramount examples of desertification resulting from irrigation schemes are found in the Aral and Caspian Sea regions, the Hei and Tarim River basins in western China, and the Senegal River basin in Africa[50]

Once the world's fourth largest lake, the Aral Sea has shrunk dramatically over the past few decades as the primary rivers that fed it have been diverted and tapped nearly dry for irrigation of farmland. By 1989, the northern and southern half of the sea had become virtually separated. The drying out of the sea's southern part exposed the salty seabed. Dust storms increased, spreading the salty soil on the agricultural lands. The water making its way back to the sea is increasingly saline and polluted by pesticides and fertilizer. In 2003, the sea's southern half had been separated into a western and eastern half.[51]

> "Irrigation has led to increased cultivation and food production in drylands, but in many cases this has been unsustainable without extensive public capital investment."

Sub-Saharan African and Central Asian drylands are among the most vulnerable to climate change

An estimated 10-20 per cent of drylands are being degraded through a reduction or loss of biological or economic productivity. Such desertification is caused by various factors, including climate variations and human activities. About 1-6 per cent of the dryland inhabitants live in desertified areas. A much larger number is under threat from desertification, which is likely to be aggravated by climate change.[52]

Several studies have been conducted on long-term environmental and agricultural change, but only of late have climatic factors been seriously taken into account. In north China, for instance, wind erosion appears to have compounded the effects of anthropogenic pressure to accelerate desertification.[53]

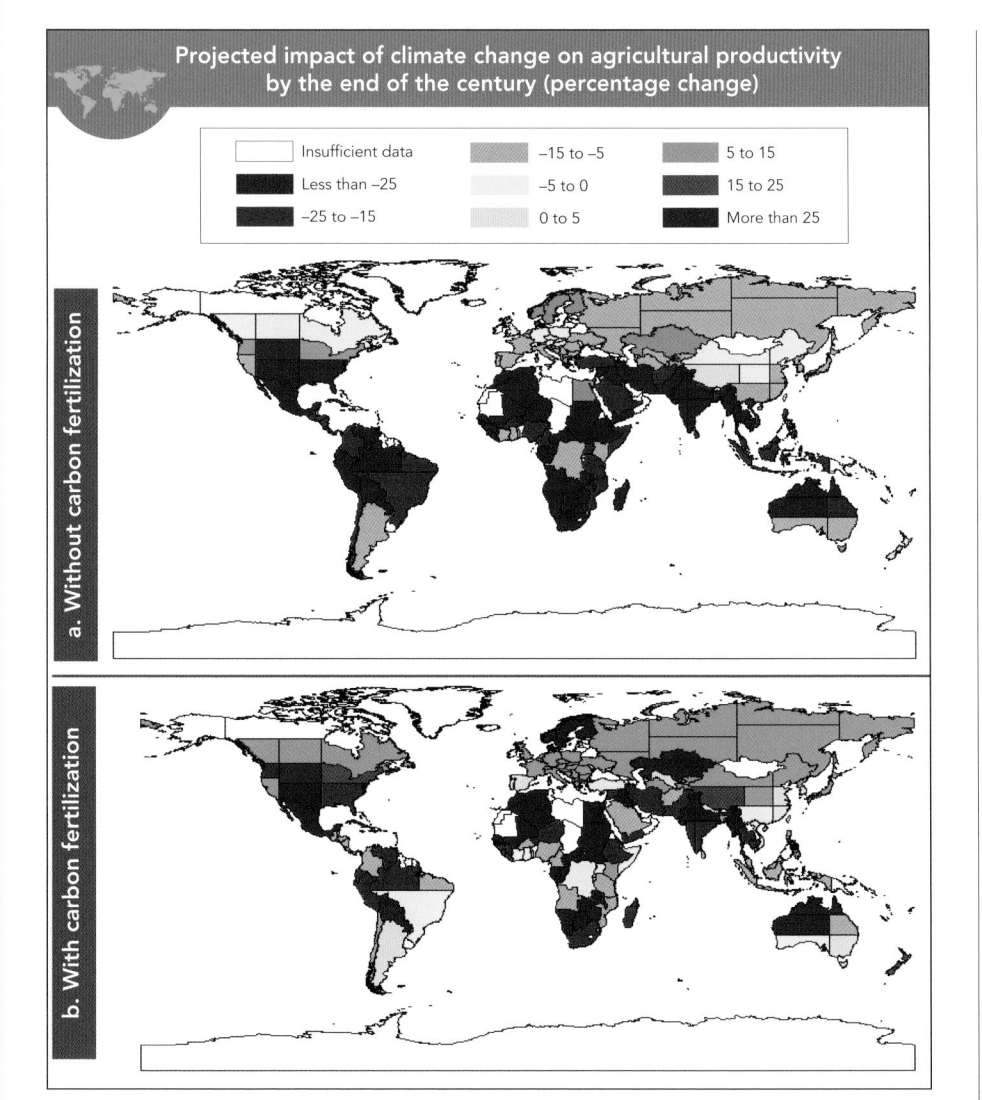

Projected impact of climate change on agricultural productivity by the end of the century (percentage change)

Legend:
- Insufficient data
- Less than −25
- −25 to −15
- −15 to −5
- −5 to 0
- 0 to 5
- 5 to 15
- 15 to 25
- More than 25

a. Without carbon fertilization

b. With carbon fertilization

Source: Cline (2007).

Note: Because the focus is on the impacts on agricultural potential, trade effects are not considered. Adaptation through shifts in planting timing and shifts to other available crops and increased irrigation using existing systems are considered to some extent.

Agricultural activity in many developing countries is likely to be adversely affected by climate change

There is still some debate regarding the extent to which climate change will affect agricultural productivity at the global level (e.g., because of uncertainty regarding the effects of higher carbon concentration on plant growth, or carbon fertilization). By one estimate, under business as usual, climate change by the 2080s would reduce world agricultural production capacity by about 16 per cent if carbon fertilization is omitted and by about 3 per cent if it is included. Other studies are more optimistic. There is, however, wide consensus that, even if a moderate increase were the outcome at the global level, there would be serious losses for many countries and regions, particularly in the developing world. For instance, it is estimated that India and a large number of countries in Africa would face major losses in crop yields even with carbon fertilization.[54]

Furthermore, the likely increase in the frequency of extreme events, such as droughts, floods and pest outbreaks (which are not considered in these projections), suggests that it would be a risky strategy to focus the response to climate change exclusively on adaptation.[55]

Endnotes

45 Millennium Ecosystem Assessment (2005), *Ecosystems and Human Well-being: Current State and Trends: Findings of the Condition and Trends Working Group*, http://www.millenniumassessment.org/en/Condition.aspx.

46 Millennium Ecosystem Assessment (2005), *Ecosystems and Human Well-being: Current State and Trends: Findings of the Condition and Trends Working Group*, http://www.millenniumassessment.org/en/Condition.aspx.

47 Millennium Ecosystem Assessment (2005), *Ecosystems and Human Well-being: Current State and Trends: Findings of the Condition and Trends Working Group*, http://www.millenniumassessment.org/en/Condition.aspx.

48 Y. Boubacar, M. Larwanou, A. Hassane and C. Reij in conjunction with International Resources Group (IRG) (2005), Etude du Sahel—Rapport Etude Pilote Niger, http://epiq2admin.web.aplus.net/pubs/niger_etude_sahel.pdf; and S. M. Herrmann, A. Anyamba and C. J. Tucker (2005), "Recent trends in vegetation dynamics in the African Sahel and their relationship to climate", *Global Environmental Change*, Part A, 15(4), pp. 394-404.

49 S. M. Herrmann, A. Anyamba and C. J. Tucker (2005), "Recent trends in vegetation dynamics in the African Sahel and their relationship to climate", *Global Environmental Change*, Part A, 15(4), pp. 394-404.

50 H. J. Geist and E. F. Lambin (2004), "Dynamic causal patterns of desertification", *BioScience*, 54(9), pp. 817-829.

51 NASA Earth Observatory, http://earthobservatory.nasa.gov.

52 Millennium Ecosystem Assessment (2005), *Ecosystems and Human Well-being: Current State and Trends: Findings of the Condition and Trends Working Group*, http://www.millenniumassessment.org/en/Condition.aspx.

53 X. Wang, F. Chen and Z. Dong (2006), "The relative role of climatic and human factors in desertification in semiarid China", *Global Environmental Change*, 16, pp. 48-57; and Y. Chen and H. Tang (2005), "Desertification in North China: Background, anthropogenic impacts and failures in combating it", *Land Degradation and Development*, 16, pp. 367-376.

54 W. R. Cline (2007), *Global Warming and Agriculture: Impact Estimates by Country*, Center for Global Development, Peterson Institute for International Economics, Washington, D.C., 186 p.; and IPCC (2007), "Food, fibre and forest products", chapter 5 in *Climate Change 2007: Impacts, Adaptation and Vulnerability*, Fourth Assessment Report.

55 W. R. Cline (2007), *Global Warming and Agriculture: Impact Estimates by Country*, Center for Global Development, Peterson Institute for International Economics, Washington, D.C., 186 p.; and IPCC (2007), "Food, fibre and forest products", chapter 5 in *Climate Change 2007: Impacts, Adaptation and Vulnerability*, Fourth Assessment Report.

Sources for graphs and maps

Millennium Ecosystem Assessment (2005), *Ecosystems and Human Well-being: Current State and Trends: Findings of the Condition and Trends Working Group*, http://www.millenniumassessment.org/en/Condition.aspx.

S. M. Herrmann, A. Anyamba and C. J. Tucker (2005), "Recent trends in vegetation dynamics in the African Sahel and their relationship to climate", *Global Environmental Change*, Part A, 15(4), pp. 394-404.

G. Tappan, USGS Data Center for EROS, South Dakota.

NASA Earth Observatory, http://earthobservatory.nasa.gov.

W. R. Cline (2007). *Global Warming and Agriculture: Impact Estimates by Country.* Center for Global Development, Peterson Institute for International Economics. Washington, D.C., 186 p.

Sources for quotes

Message to the International Conference on Combating Desertification, Beijing, 22-24 January 2008, http://www.unccd.int/documents/sgmsgbeijing.pdf.

Millennium Ecosystem Assessment (2005), *Ecosystems and Human Well-being: Desertification Synthesis*, p. 2, http://www.millenniumassessment.org/documents/document.355.aspx.pdf.

Millennium Ecosystem Assessment (2005), *Ecosystems and Human Well-being: Desertification Synthesis*, p. 10, http://www.millenniumassessment.org/documents/document.355.aspx.pdf.

DROUGHT

Droughts often result in heavy crop damage and livestock losses, disrupt energy production and hurt ecosystems. They cover wide areas of land and often affect several neighbouring regions or countries simultaneously. Droughts can lead to famines, loss of life, mass migration and conflict. Hence, droughts can wipe out development gains and accumulated wealth in developing countries, especially for the poorest.[56]

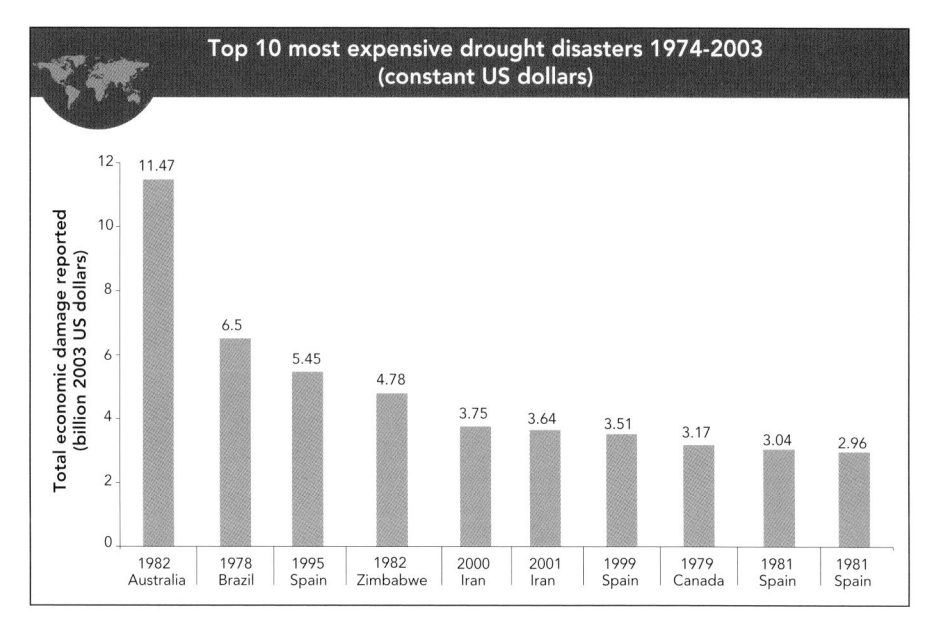

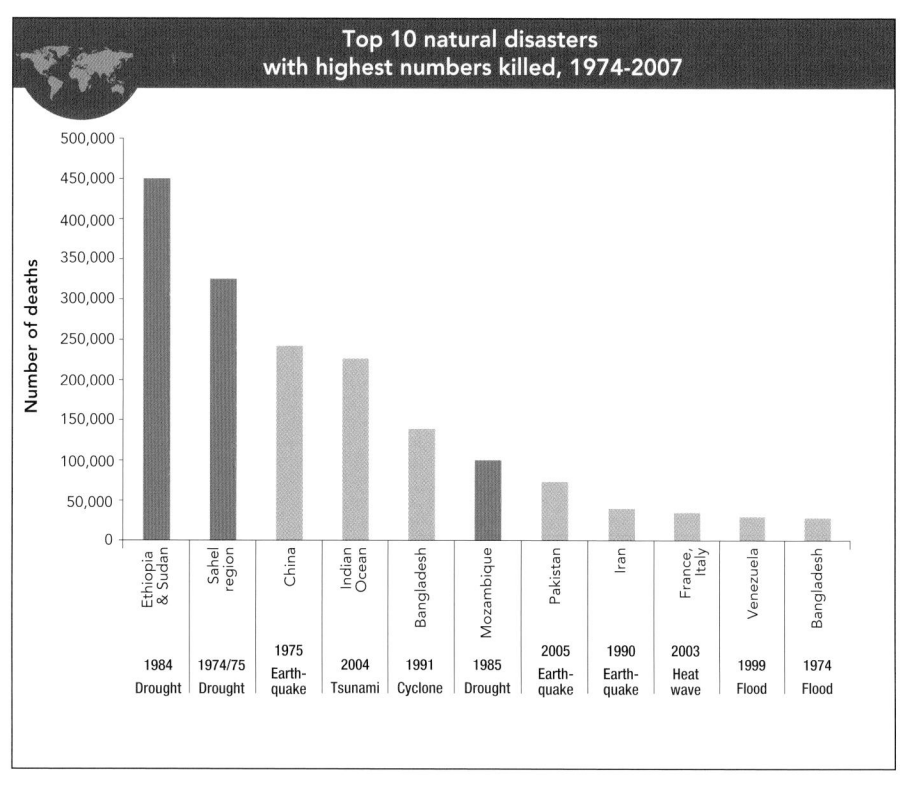

Top 10 natural disasters with highest numbers killed, 1974-2007

Location	Year	Event	Number of deaths (approx.)
Ethiopia & Sudan	1984	Drought	450,000
Sahel region	1974/75	Drought	325,000
China	1975	Earthquake	242,000
Indian Ocean	2004	Tsunami	227,000
Bangladesh	1991	Cyclone	138,000
Mozambique	1985	Drought	100,000
Pakistan	2005	Earthquake	73,000
Iran	1990	Earthquake	40,000
France, Italy	2003	Heat wave	35,000
Venezuela	1999	Flood	30,000
Bangladesh	1974	Flood	27,000

Source: Guha-Sapir, Hargitt and Hoyois (2004) and EM-DAT, the OFDA/CRED International Disaster Database.

Top 10 most expensive drought disasters 1974-2003 (constant US dollars)

Total economic damage reported (billion 2003 US dollars)

Year	Location	Damage
1982	Australia	11.47
1978	Brazil	6.5
1995	Spain	5.45
1982	Zimbabwe	4.78
2000	Iran	3.75
2001	Iran	3.64
1999	Spain	3.51
1979	Canada	3.17
1981	Spain	3.04
1981	Spain	2.96

Source: Guha-Sapir, Hargitt and Hoyois (2004).

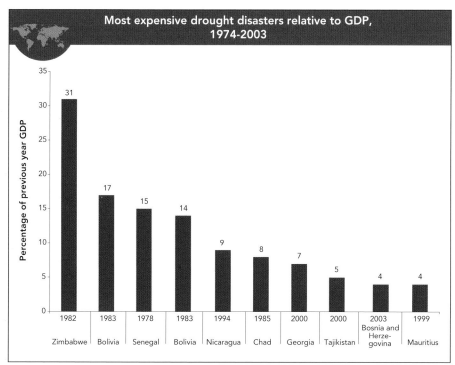

Most expensive drought disasters relative to GDP, 1974-2003

Year	Country	Percentage
1982	Zimbabwe	31
1983	Bolivia	17
1978	Senegal	15
1983	Bolivia	14
1994	Nicaragua	9
1985	Chad	8
2000	Georgia	7
2000	Tajikistan	5
2003	Bosnia and Herzegovina	4
1999	Mauritius	4

Source: Guha-Sapir, Hargitt and Hoyois (2004).

Drought mortality is concentrated in developing countries, while absolute economic losses are largest in developed regions

In relative terms, developing countries are those suffering the biggest economic losses. In a number of countries, drought wiped out significantly more than 5 per cent of the previous year's GDP.

Unlike earthquakes, droughts can be predictable, usually developing over several years. This makes it possible to respond to droughts as they occur. Several regional early warning systems, such as the Famine Early Warning System that covers Africa, have been set up around the world for this purpose.[57]

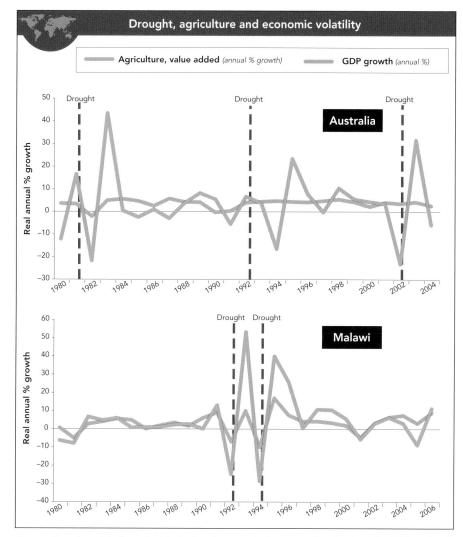

Drought, agriculture and economic volatility

Source: Based on data from the World Development Indicators online database for GDP and agricultural value added real annual growth rates and from EM-DAT, the OFDA/CRED International Disaster Database, for years of drought.

Developing country economies are especially vulnerable to droughts

Periodic droughts affect both developing and developed countries, with direct impacts on agriculture and on other productive sectors reliant on water, such as hydroelectricity. It is in developing countries, however, where drought is highly correlated with the performance of the overall economy, as a result of heavy reliance on agriculture. Not only does water variability significantly reduce projected rates of economic growth in vulnerable countries, but it has a dramatic effect on poverty rates. At the same time, poor transport infrastructure exacerbates the inability of local economies to adjust to localized crop failures, as it hinders food surpluses from reaching areas in food deficit.[58]

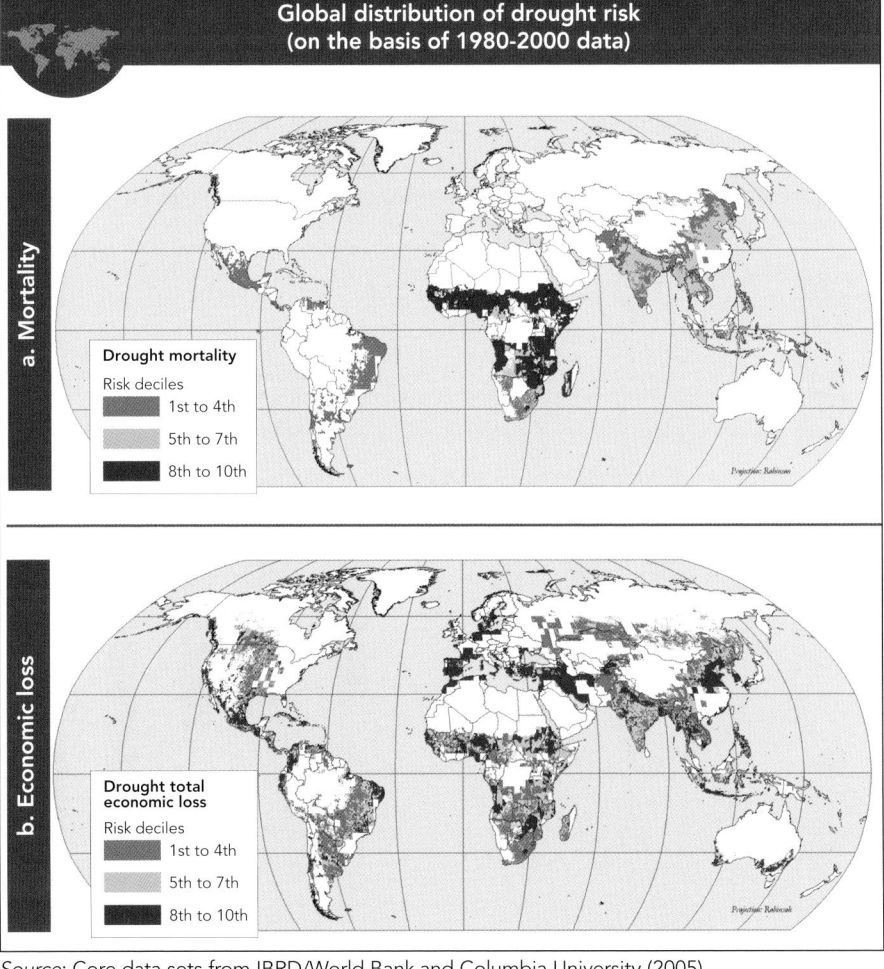

Global distribution of drought risk
(on the basis of 1980-2000 data)

a. Mortality

Drought mortality

Risk deciles

1st to 4th

5th to 7th

8th to 10th

b. Economic loss

Drought total economic loss

Risk deciles

1st to 4th

5th to 7th

8th to 10th

Source: Core data sets from IBRD/World Bank and Columbia University (2005).

Note: Sparsely populated areas and those without significant agricultural activity are excluded from the analysis and appear as white areas in the maps. The global risks of mortality and economic losses resulting from drought were assessed by combining hazard exposure with historical vulnerability, considering population density and GDP per unit area.

Drought mortality hot spots are concentrated in sub-Saharan Africa, but economic loss hot spots are located in several relatively developed regions

Regional differences in loss risks are in part due to differences in population density, in the size of the areas affected and in the degree of hazard across regions. But they also reflect differences in vulnerability. For instance, droughts in Africa tend to result in high mortality rates due to the generally low level of preparedness.[59]

The expanded UN Central Emergency Response Fund (CERF), launched in 2006 as a standby fund to enable more timely and reliable humanitarian assistance to those affected by natural disasters and armed conflicts, is one example of a more proactive approach to disaster risk management.[60] In the cases where risk cannot be adequately addressed through risk mitigation measures, some countries have used other risk management strategies, such as risk insurance. For instance, weather-index-based insurance to manage drought risk has been piloted in several countries with success.[61]

> **Desertification has its greatest impact in Africa, where some two thirds of the continent are covered by desert and drylands, and are afflicted by frequent and severe droughts.**
>
> —Michel Jarraud
> WMO Secretary-General

Endnotes

56 D. Guha-Sapir, D. Hargitt and P. Hoyois (2004), *Thirty Years of Natural Disasters 1974-2003: The Numbers*, Presses Universitaires de Louvain: Louvain-la-Neuve.

57 A. Kreimer, M. Arnold and A. Carlin (2003), *Building Safer Cities: The Future of Disaster Risk*, Disaster Risk Management Series, No. 3, World Bank.

58 E. Clay, L. Bohn, E. Blanco de Armas, S. Kabambe and H. Tchale (2003), "Malawi and Southern Africa: climatic variability and economic performance", Disaster Risk Management Working Paper Series No. 7, World Bank, Washington, D.C., http://unfccc.int/files/cooperation_and_support/capacity_building/application/pdf/wbmalawi.pdf; and World Bank (2006), "Managing water resources to maximize sustainable growth: a World Bank water resources assistance strategy for Ethiopia", a Country Water Resources Assistance Strategy, World Bank, Washington, D.C.

59 IBRD, World Bank and Columbia University (2005), Natural disaster hotspots: a global risk analysis—synthesis report, http://sedac.ciesin.columbia.edu/hazards/hotspots/synthesisreport.pdf.

60 ISDR (2007), "Disaster risk reduction: 2007 global review", consultation edition, prepared for the Global Platform for Disaster Risk Reduction, first session, Geneva, Switzerland, 5-7 June 2007, ISDR/GP/2007/3.

61 J. Syroka and E. Bryla (2007), "Developing index-based insurance for agriculture in developing countries", *Sustainable Development Innovation Briefs*, No. 2, March, http://www.un.org/esa/sustdev/publications/innovationbriefs/no2.pdf.

Sources for graphs and maps

D. Guha-Sapir, D. Hargitt and P. Hoyois (2004), *Thirty Years of Natural Disasters 1974-2003: The Numbers*, Presses Universitaires de Louvain: Louvain-la-Neuve.

EM-DAT, OFDA/CRED International Disaster Database, Université Catholique de Louvain, Brussels, Belgium, http://www.em-dat.net.

World Development Indicators online database, http://devdata.worldbank.org/dataonline.

IBRD/World Bank and Columbia University (2005), Natural disaster hotspots: a global risk analysis: core data sets, http://www.ldeo.columbia.edu/chrr/research/hotspots/coredata.html

Source for quote

M. Jarraud (2006), The Secretary-General of the World Meteorological Organization Stresses the Importance of Preparedness, Press Release WMO-No.707, http://www.wmo.int/web/Press/Press707.doc.

Library Network
University of Ottawa
Date Due

Réseau de bibliothèques
Université d'Ottawa
Échéance